FABRICRAFTS

FABRICRAFTS

50 Extraordinary Gifts and Projects, Step by Step

Gillian Souter

CROWN TRADE PAPERBACKS

New York

Published by Crown Trade Paperbacks, 201 East 50th Street, New York,
New York 10022. Member of the Crown Publishing Group.

Random House, Inc. New York, Toronto, London, Sydney, Auckland

CROWN TRADE PAPBERBACKS and colophon are trademarks of
Crown Publishers, Inc.

Originally published in Australia by Off the Shelf Publishing in 1996.

Printed in China

LIBRARY OF CONGRESS CATALOGING-IN-PUBLICATION DATA
is available upon request.

ISBN 0-517-88532-8

10 9 8 7 6 5 4 3 2 1

First American Edition

Foreword

Fabric has always had a special role in our lives. From the times when the arts of weaving and felting were developed and humans were no longer dependent on animal skins for warmth, we have found exciting and unusual ways to decorate and use fabric. In many cultures, fabrics signified status either by color, type of fiber, or by the form of embellishment. Today, we have such an abundance of choice that we can select anything from rich velvets to rustic muslins to create an effect, and the potential for crafting with fabric is as unlimited as our imaginations.

Even those of us who didn't pay enough attention while sitting at our mother's feet, there is little that you need to learn before working with fabrics. Basic techniques are covered in the introductory chapter of this book. The chapters which follow introduce some of the extraordinary ways in which fabric can be made, shaped or decorated. For each method, you'll find a brief overview, along with three stunning projects, including:

A personal item, ideal as a gift

Something useful for the home

Items for special occasions

There are also ideas for wrapping gifts and tips on making greeting cards and gift tags, so that you can share the enjoyment you've had in crafting your own gifts from fabric.

Contents

Fabrics 8

Equipment 10

Basic Techniques 12

Weaving 16

Feltcraft 24

Scrapcraft 32

Canvaswork 40

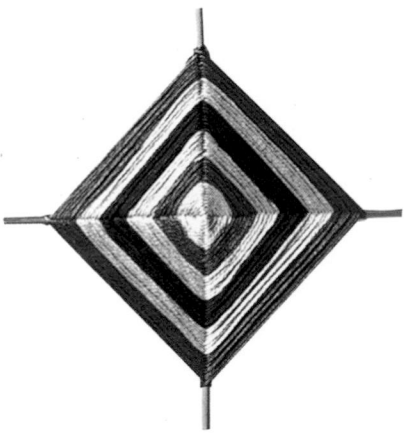

Ribbon & Lace 48

Patchwork 56

Appliqué 64

Quilting 72

Fabric Sculpture 80

Cartonnage 88

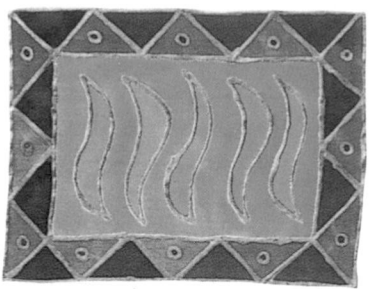

Painting 96

Dyeing 104

Marbling 112

Printing 120

Stenciling 128

Embroidery 136

Beadwork 144

Gift Giving 152

Patterns 156

Index 160

Fabrics

Fabric is formed by interweaving the fibers of raw materials. Those made from natural fibers, such as silk, cotton, linen, or wool, have quite different properties to synthetic fabrics. In general, natural fibers are more absorbent and porous which means that they absorb paint better and are more prone to creasing. Some, including cotton and silk, will weaken when exposed to sunlight.

There are several other considerations when selecting a fabric for a project. The weight, color and patterning are all factors. A furnishing fabric will probably not be flexible or light enough for making a scarf, and a fine silk will have a limited life in the play room.

If you are planning to dabble in fabric crafts, a collection of different fabrics is invaluable. Rummage through the remnant baskets at fabric stores. Ask manufacturers or wholesalers whether they have any samples they no longer want. Keep scraps left over from making clothes and furnishings, as even the smallest piece can prove useful later on. Such pieces are only useful, however, if you can locate them when the time comes. Take care, too, not to buy fabrics just for the sake of hoarding.

Backing and lining fabrics, although less important, are needed for many projects. Keep a supply of thin cottons for lining and match pale top fabrics with pale linings, and dark with dark.

Natural fabrics, such as cotton and silk, often give the most pleasing results.

Felt is available in a range of colors and is ideal for children's fabric crafts as it does not fray.

Unusual fabrics, such as velvet and satin, can give a rich effect but are more difficult to work with.

Fabrics printed with a pattern can add life to a project.

Fabrics with an even weave, such as Aida and some types of linen, are essential for counted embroidery.

Equipment

Most fabric stores offer a bewildering array of gimmicks and knick-knacks designed to complicate your approach to fabric crafts. There is, however, no need to outlay large amounts of money and you probably have most of the necessary items in your sewing basket from childhood.

If the old ones have rusted, you may need to purchase a new set of needles. These come in various shapes and sizes, but the main choices are the size of head and the sharpness of the point.

Transparent paper from the kitchen will be needed for tracing patterns, or you can buy heavier paper from an art supplies store. Fabric paints are available in ready-mixed colors. Alternatively, you can buy a textile medium and add it to most acrylic paints to make them suitable for fabrics.

A sewing machine will speed up much of the basic sewing required but all stitching can be done by hand, if necessary.

Equipment and materials needed for each project are listed in a box above the project picture. If you don't have a specified item, read the instructions and you may find that an alternative will do just as well. When the list includes "sewing equipment" the project will probably require a tape measure, fabric scissors, a suitable needle, and thread in a color to match the fabric.

Counterclockwise:
bias binding; polyester wadding and fiber filler; piping cord and decorative cord; needles; embroidery scissors; fabric scissors; machine foot and bobbins; a thimble; a pin cushion; a paint brush and palette; a tape measure.

Basic Techniques

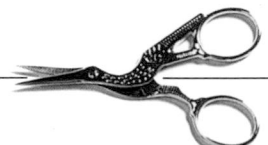

There are no mysteries to the techniques used in this book. Many of them were learned in your first sewing lesson at school. If you had a traditional boy's upbringing and weren't given that opportunity, a sewing book for children will fill the gap!

Sewing, however, is a small part of the projects in this book. The processes of forming fabrics, shaping them, and decorating them involve quite an array of techniques, but none of them are especially complex. Anything unusual that you need to know is discussed in the opening pages of each chapter and it is worthwhile reading through that text before undertaking the relevant projects. These projects offer a starting point and will hopefully encourage you to explore techniques which catch your interest.

Understanding Fabric

Woven fabric is basically a mesh of two sets of yarns: warp and weft. A firmly woven strip known as selvage is formed along each lengthwise edge. Grains indicate the direction of the yarn: the lengthwise grain is that of the warp, the crosswise grain is that of the weft. A bias is any diagonal intersecting these two grain lines, but true bias is at a 45° angle to any straight edge.

Lengthwise grain has very little stretch in it, whereas crosswise has a little more, and bias the most of all. This affects how the fabric will drape when hung and how it will lie in a curved seam.

When cutting fabric, it is important that the scissor blades are very sharp, or they will drag the fibers and spoil the fabric.

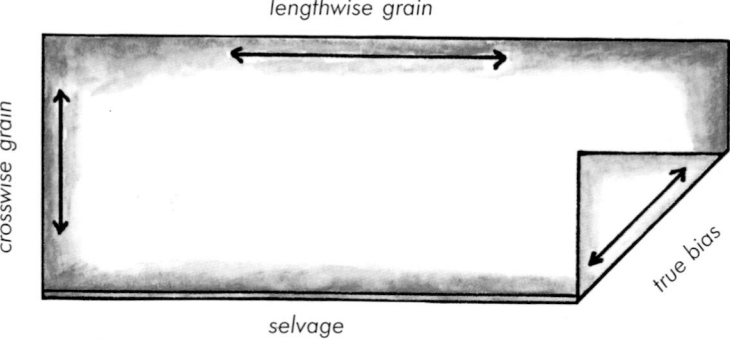

lengthwise grain

crosswise grain

true bias

selvage

Straightening Ends

It may be necessary to straighten the ends of a piece of fabric before you can check it for grain alignment. The fastest method, and one suitable only for firmly woven fabrics, is to snip into the selvage and then tear it. For loosely woven or soft fabrics, snip the selvage and gently pull a thread, then cut along the gap left by the pulled thread.

Preventing Fraying

Some fabrics fray more readily than others. This, plus the number of times an item will be washed and whether much strain will be put on its seams all determine whether or not you should try to prevent edges from fraying.

The simplest method is to cut the fabric with pinking shears. Another method is to staystitch or zigzag along the edge with a sewing machine. This is more secure but creates a bulkier seam and some fabrics may pucker.

Fray-prevention liquid, which is basically glue, is useful for dabbing on small areas, such as snipped seams or turned corners.

Prewashing

Fabrics are often treated with a size or coating after they have been manufactured and if you plan to apply paint or dye, you will need to wash the fabric thoroughly first. Use plain soap and, if possible, allow the fabric to soak in soapy water for an hour or so before rinsing it well and hanging it up to dry. Press the dry fabric well to remove any creases.

Transferring Patterns

There are various means of transferring patterns onto fabric; your choice depends on the fabric color and how the design will be worked. Use tracing paper to copy the pattern from this book and then mark the fabric with tailor's chalk, a dissolvable marker or a soft lead pencil. Tape the pattern and fabric to a window and then trace the lines.

Scaling Patterns

Some of the patterns in this book will need to be enlarged. Scaling or resizing a pattern is easy to do if you have access to a photocopying machine. If you don't, you can use the squaring up method described below.

If the instructions in a project say to enlarge a pattern by 200%, you will need to double its size. 300% would be three times the size of the printed pattern, and so on.

◄ *To enlarge a pattern by hand, use the squaring up method. Trace the pattern and rule a ½ " grid over it. If the instructions specify to enlarge it by 200%, rule a 1 " grid on a fresh piece of tracing paper and copy the pattern, square by square.*

Basic Sewing

None of the projects in this book requires any difficult sewing techniques. If you have a sewing machine, this will speed up the laborious aspects of sewing. Some handsewing is often required to complete projects, and you may prefer to work all the sewing by hand on smaller items.

A hem is a finish for a fabric edge and can be simply turned up, faced, or enclosed by turning twice. Your choice depends on the project's use. Casing, a fabric tunnel made to enclose a drawstring, is much like an enclosed hem but with an extra row of stitching along the edge.

Seams hold two pieces of fabric together. Generally, seam allowances should be no less than ¼ " and not too wide, or the seam will be bulky and unattractive. On curved seams, the allowance will need to be snipped close to the line of stitching so that the seam will lie flat when turned.

n an outward curve, noving wedges m the seam allowce will give a oother finish.

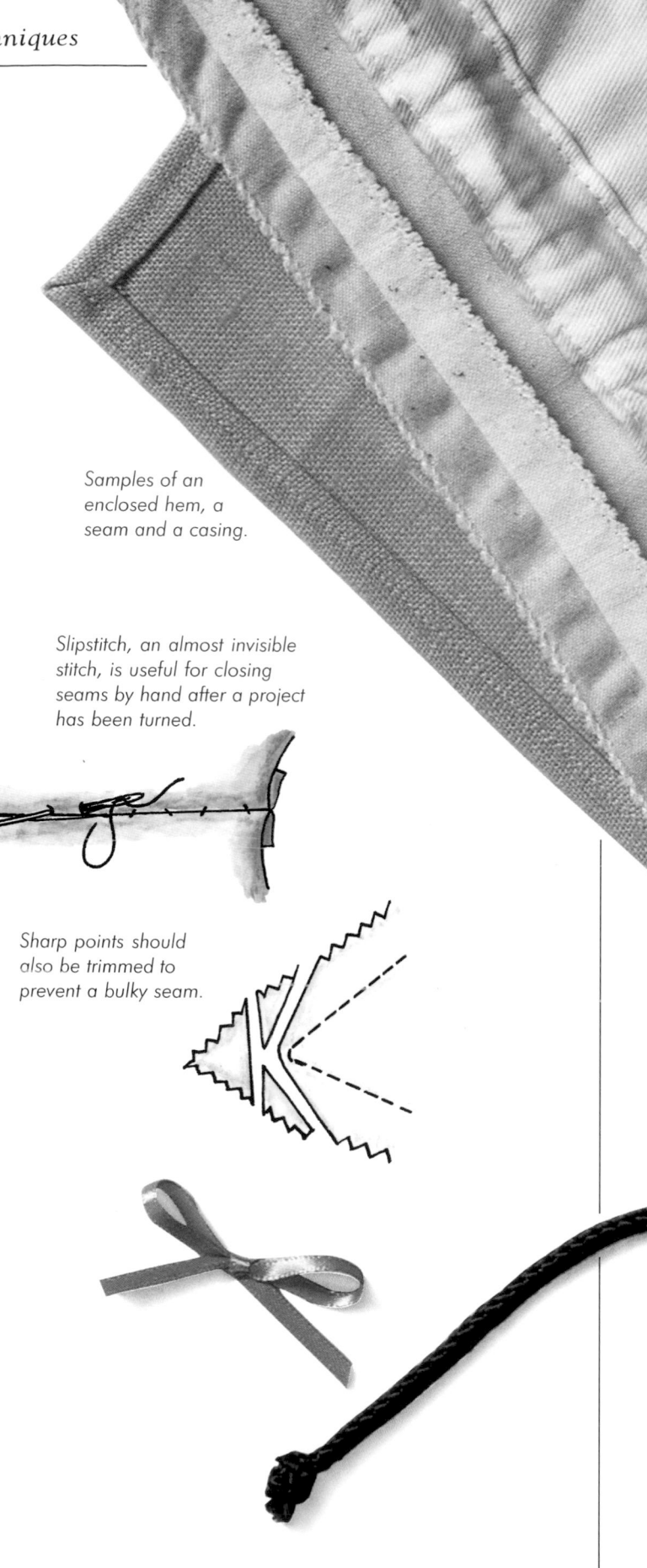

Samples of an enclosed hem, a seam and a casing.

Slipstitch, an almost invisible stitch, is useful for closing seams by hand after a project has been turned.

Sharp points should also be trimmed to prevent a bulky seam.

Finishing Touches

Close attention to the smaller details will make your fabric project even more special. A good supply of ribbons, cords and yarns will give mean you can add such touches without making a special trip to the store.

To prevent the ends of cords from unravelling, knot them tightly or dip them in white glue. Bows can be stitched in place so they hold their shape. Instructions for making small tassels appear on page 85.

Weaving

Weaving, interlacing threads to form cloth, is one of the most natural of crafts and one which humans have enjoyed since time immemorial. The craft has its own extensive set of terms which, in English, have been preserved from Anglo-Saxon. To the uninitiated, they are mere jargon; to the enthusiastic weaver, words such as "warp" and "woof" are dear to the heart.

All woven fabric is made of a set of warp threads which have another set of threads, the weft, running across them in over-and-under variations. The threads can be made of wool, string, raffia or anything you please: different threads will give different effects. Thicker yarns give a result sooner, finer ones allow more detail in design.

A loom needed to weave large pieces of fabric can be both cumbersome and expensive. Instead, you can make your own loom from a picture frame, some cardboard, or simply by using your own body. Back-strap or waist weaving is found in many cultures, from Lapland to Guatemala. The long strips that it produces can be used as they are, or sewn together to form wider cloths.

The most useful tools associated with weaving can be made at home. A shuttle, a rectangle with notches cut at each end, is used to feed the weft yarn through the warp threads. A heddle is a means of raising or lowering warp threads to allow the shuttle to be fed through quickly. This can be a simple ruler, as used in Project 3. If you are using a picture frame for a loom, the heddle can be a more complex affair, with alternating slits and eyes, which allows movement up and down. A comb, or "beater" is also useful for packing down the weft threads as you work.

This chapter includes some very basic projects, designed to introduce different methods of weaving. After further research, you might want to try more ambitious projects.

A simple shuttle allows you to feed the yarn more easily.

Woven variations
Different patterns can be obtained simply by changing the sequence of the weft.
Right: a plain or tabby weave, with an over-and-under-one balanced warp and weft.
Far right: a herringbone pattern, woven by varying the jumps of the weft.

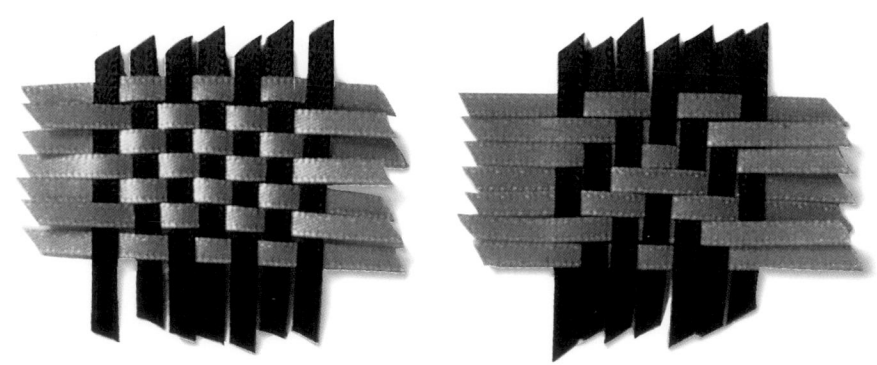

Friendship bands, made to be worn around the wrist, are especially popular with children. They originate from South America, and are made with brightly colored embroidery threads.

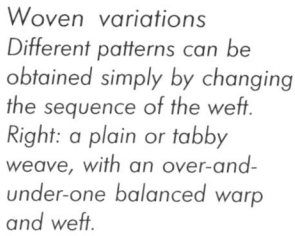

Back-strap weaving can be used to make belts, bookmarks, and even braces. Once proficient, you can weave letters and patterns.

▲ To make a simple loom, cut a piece of very stiff cardboard, longer and wider than the desired size of the finished weaving. Mark a line ½ " from each end and mark a series of dots at regular intervals (such as ¼ "). Snip into the cardboard at these points, cutting notches to the marked line.

Tie one end of a ball of string to the first tab and wind it around the loom, slipping it into the next notch at each end. Secure the end of the string around the last tab.

PROJECT 1

Ojos Mobile

YOU WILL NEED
wooden skewers
cotton or wool
scissors
glue
a needle

Ojos or "eyes" are traditionally made in Mexico for young children: the number of colors represents the age of the child. Here, several ojos are combined to form a mobile.

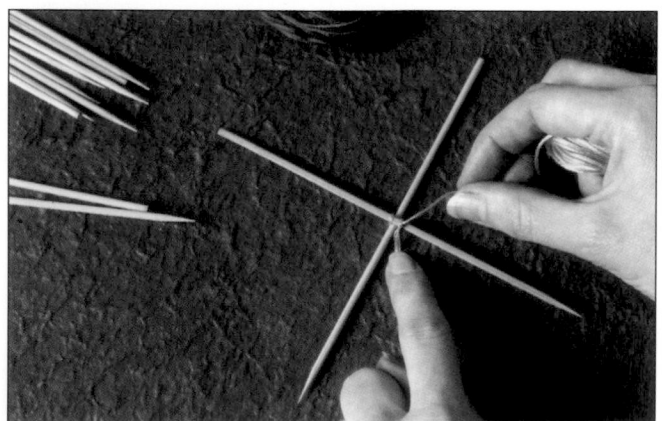

1 Make five small ojos as follows. Bind two small wooden skewers tightly with yarn to form a cross. You can use a ball of wool or a skein of embroidery cotton as shown here. Lay the scrap end of the yarn along one spoke; it will be covered by the weaving yarn.

2 Wind the yarn from one spoke to the next, back around the spoke, and then on to the next one. Maintain an even tension as you work around the cross.

3 To change colors, bring the first yarn behind a spoke and knot it to the second yarn. Lay the scrap end of the first yarn along the spoke and continue weaving with the second yarn. When the ojo is complete, secure the yarn with a knot and a dab of glue and leave a length of yarn for hanging the ojo.

4 Using two long skewers, make another ojo from which to hang the five small ones. Trim the sharp ends of all the skewers. Suspend a small ojo from each spoke of the large ojo and another from the center. Thread a loop of yarn through the center for hanging the finished mobile.

PROJECT 2

Bookmark

A bookmark is an ideal project to make when you embark on back-strap weaving. Don't worry if the result looks a little rough—that will be part of its charm!

YOU WILL NEED
colored yarn
stiff cardboard
a knife & mat
a ruler
a hole punch
scissors
a comb
a tapestry needle

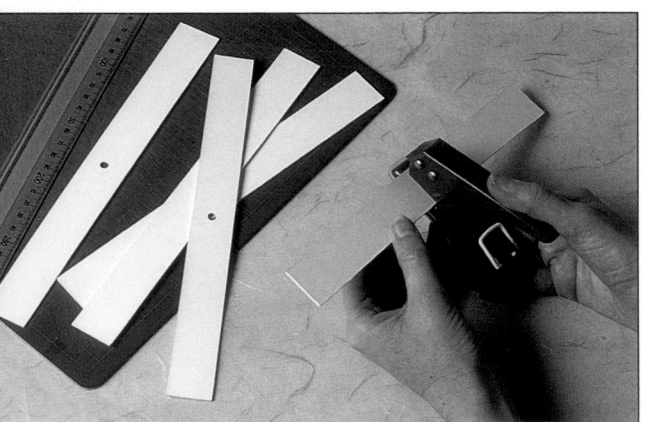

1 Measure and cut five 1 x 10 " strips of cardboard. Use a hole punch or a sharp implement to pierce a hole in the middle of each card. Cut 13 lengths of yarn in one color, each measuring 18 ". The yarn used in the example is pearl cotton.

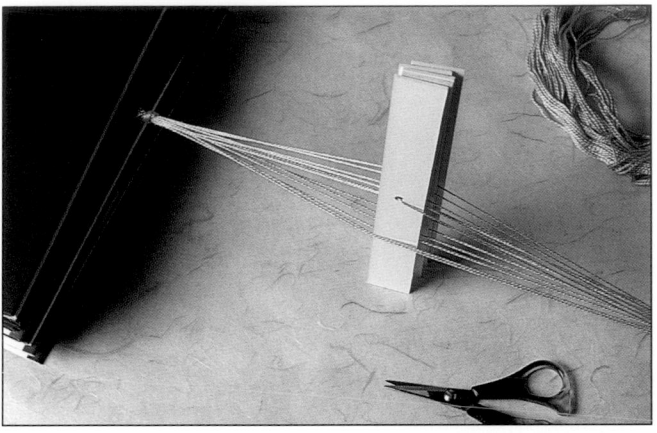

2 Tie the ends of the cut yarn with an overhand knot and secure this onto a fixed surface. With the other ends, thread one through each card, another between each card, and two at each edge. Knot the loose ends together and secure this to your belt.

3 Press all the cards down with one hand and pass a contrasting yarn through the gap, leaving a short tail at one edge. Push the cards up to raise a different set of warp threads and pass the yarn through the gap again. Continue weaving, occasionally packing down these weft threads with a comb. Change colors as you choose.

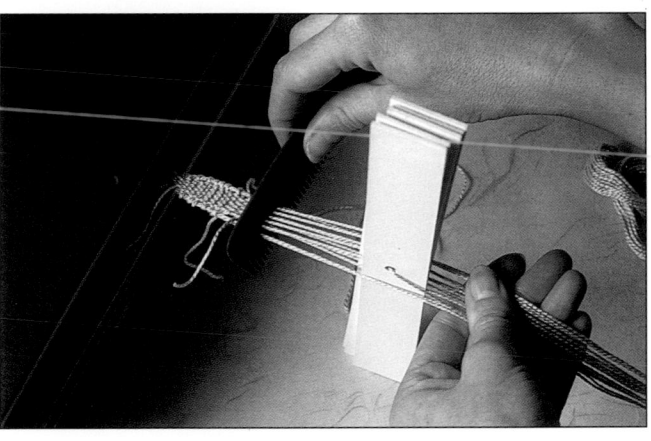

4 When the weaving is the desired length, cut the warp threads at either end. Tie these ends with a series of overhand knots: in threes at each edge and the remainder in twos. Use a large needle to thread the tail ends back into the weaving. Trim the fringes and press the bookmark flat.

PROJECT 3

Placemats

A simple cardboard loom is a wonderful way to create table mats to your own taste. This one is made with 14-ply wool in contrasting colors, but you can experiment to great effect.

YOU WILL NEED
stiff cardboard
a pencil
a ruler
a knife & mat
a ball of string
heavy ply wool
scissors
a tapestry needle
a comb

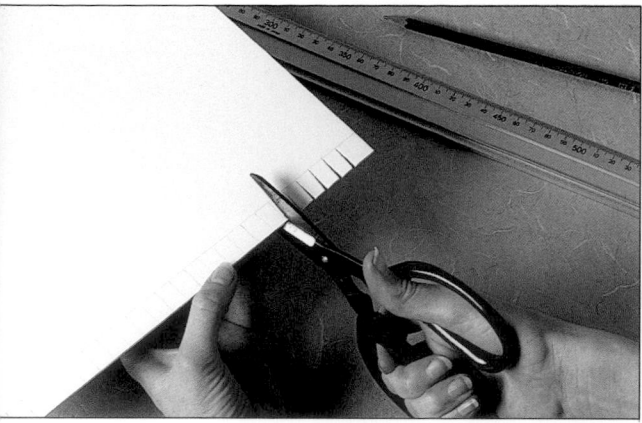

1 Measure and cut a cardboard loom for the size of mat required (see page 7). Cut a cardboard shuttle and wind onto it as much of the wool as will fit: if you want to create stripes of an even thickness, it would be wise to measure the length of this first shuttle-load.

2 Tie one end of the string securely around a corner of the loom. Wind the string around the loom, threading it through each of the slots at the top and base until it is completely threaded: this set of strings is called the warp. Weave a ruler through the warp: under one string and over the next.

3 Twist the ruler so that every alternate warp string is raised and thread the shuttle through the gap, leaving a short tail at one edge. The wool forms the weft. Twist the ruler again so that the warp lies flat and weave the shuttle under and over in the opposite sequence to your first row. Raise the warp and thread the shuttle through again. Continue until the band of color is the desired width.

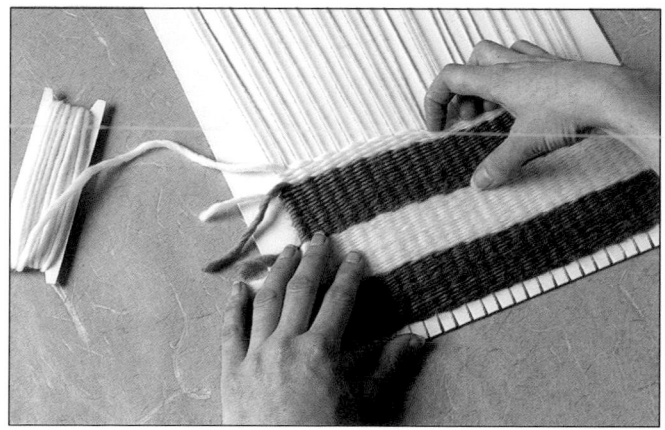

4 As you work, beat the weft down with a wide-toothed comb, or with your fingers. This will give you more working space on the loom and will produce a tighter, stronger weave. Change colors as you wish, always leaving a loose end at the edge at the start and finish of each length of wool.

5 When the mat is the desired size, cut the strings at the back of the loom. Tie the warp strings in pairs close to the edges of the weft with an overhand knot. When all the strings are knotted in pairs, trim them to create a fringe. Thread the loose ends of the weft wool into the mat with a tapestry needle.

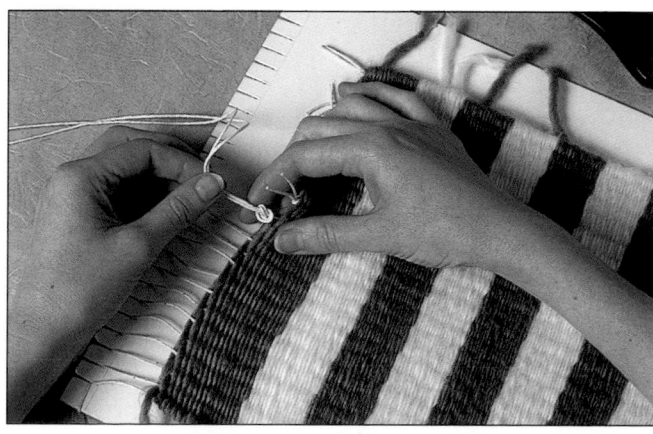

Felt Craft

Folk lore has it that Noah, for the sake of comfort, padded the floor of his ark with sheep's wool. After forty days of damp weather and animal perambulation, the loose wool had become quite matted and the world had discovered felt. True or not, felt is an ancient textile which, in northern countries, was relied on for warmth and survival. In Siberia and Scandinavia, archaeologists have found items of felt clothing dating back thousands of years. In Mongolia, felt had many uses, including home insulation.

Felt is a fabric made of wool, fur or hair which has been matted rather than spun and woven. For most of us, animal hair and fur are less readily available, so wool is most likely the material you will use. No special equipment or tools are needed in the felting process, and the result is a woollen fabric which won't fray, is easy to sew, and which will keep the wearer warm.

Wool fibers are actually covered with overlapping scales; the more scales, the easier the wool is to dye and to spin. It is generally bought in "rolags" or rolls of cleaned and carded fibers. As a rough guide, 4 oz of wool will make an 18 " square of felt. Instructions for felting are given on the next page.

Homemade felt will be thicker and less even than the machined pieces you buy. Its thickness makes homemade felt suitable for slippers and hats, while commercial felt, available in a wide array of colors, is good for detailed appliqué projects, as intricate shapes can be cut and glued in place. The fact that it does not fray makes it an ideal fabric for children to work with. Seams can be made with large stitches which become a feature of the project, especially if a contrasting color of thread is used.

Felt, either homemade or bought, can also be used for printing blocks as it absorbs paint and can be cut and mounted onto heavy cardboard. You may need to use several layers of felt if it is very thin.

You can buy wool, in natural colors or already dyed, from specialist stores or by mail order.

Felt is easy to appliqué as small pieces can simply be glued in place.

1 To make your own felt, you will need some nylon netting, rolags (rolls of carded wool), and strong thread. Cut two pieces of netting, larger than the desired piece of felt. Layer the rolags on a piece of netting, overlapping them at the edges. Lay another layer perpendicular to the first, and a third perpendicular to that.

2 Check that there are no thin patches and then lay the other piece of netting on top. Using long stitches, sew around the edges of this batt with a strong thread. Next, sew from one corner to the opposite one, across the wool. Stitch parallel rows, approximately 3 " apart. Place the batt in a tub and pour boiling water on top.

3 Wearing rubber gloves, rub soap into the batt and knead it. Roll over the batt with a rolling pin in all directions and on both sides until it is quite flat. Once the wool is firm, remove the batt from the netting and continue the hardening process. Rinse the batt well, roll it in a towel to remove the moisture and allow it to dry.

Felt and florist's wire were used to make this bright poinsettia.

PROJECT 4

Cutlery Roll

*Felt offers good protection for sharp or precious implements.
This basic project could be adapted to hold knitting needles,
pencils or other similar items.*

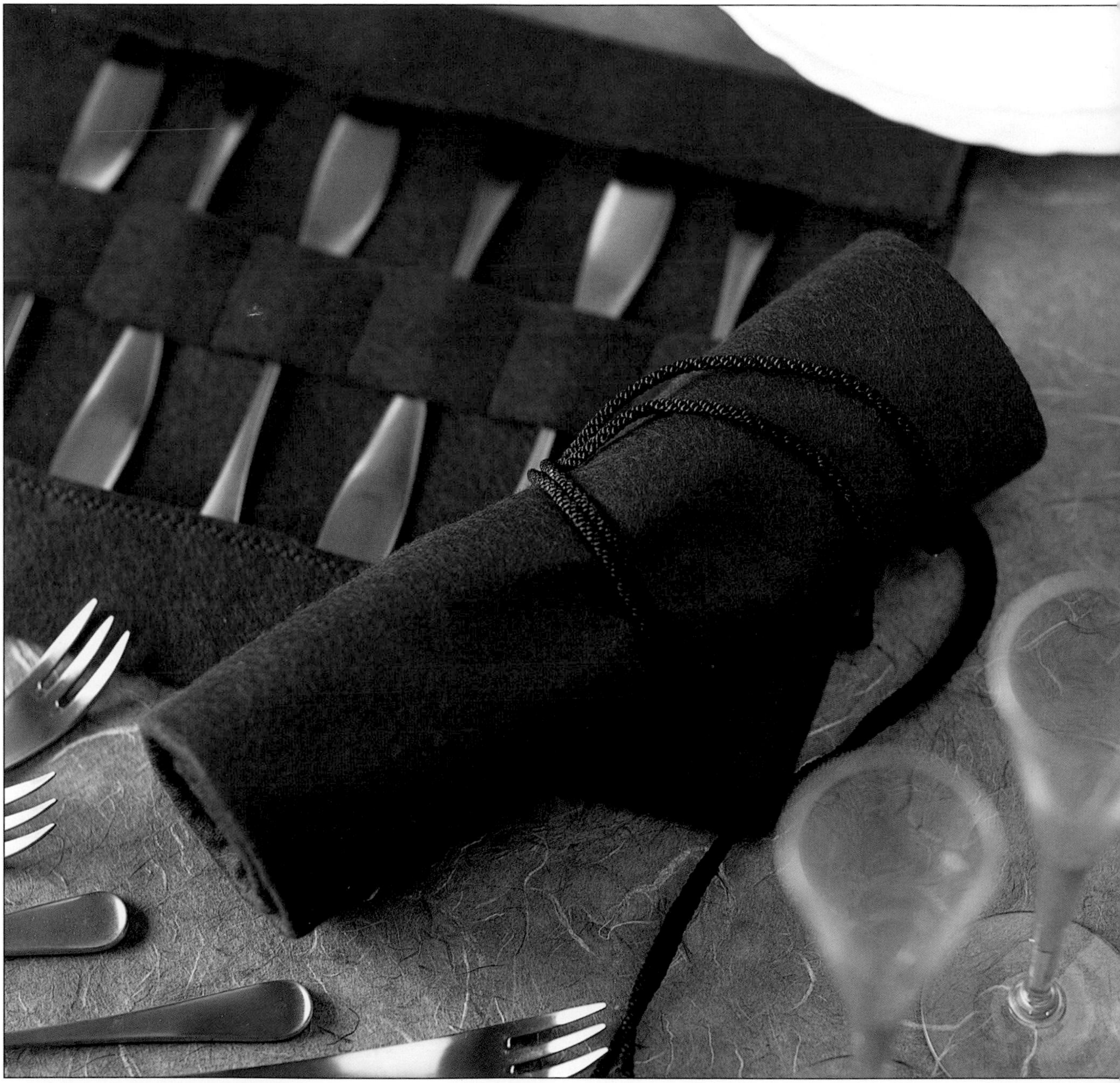

1 Measure out two pieces of felt, each 14 x 12 ", and a single strip 1½ x 12 ". Cut the pieces, using masking tape as a guide to give you straight edges.

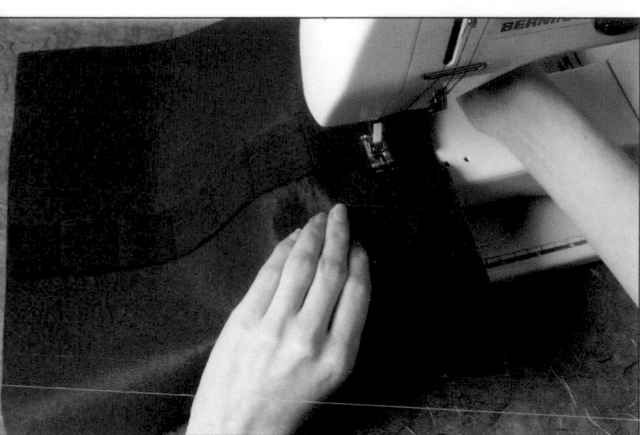

2 Place the strip along the center of one large piece of felt. Measure and pin 1½ " in from one end of the strip, then measure and pin 1½ " from there. Continue marking out spaces until you reach the other end. Sew the strip in place at the pin marks, leaving both ends unstitched.

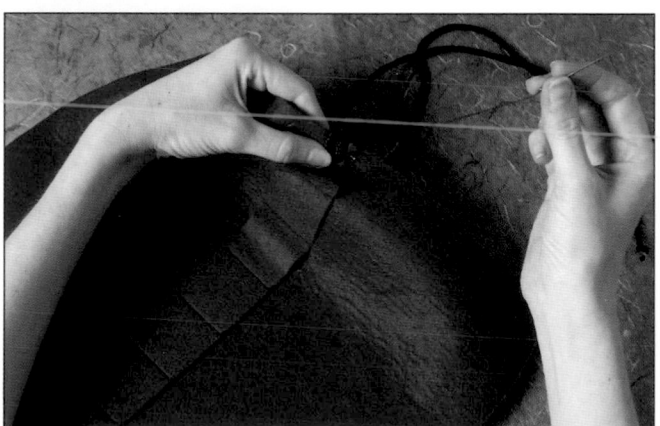

3 Cut 32 " of cord. Knot each end tightly and trim off any excess. Pin the cord between the main piece and one end of the center strip. Handsew the cord in place.

4 Pin the backing section behind the main piece and zigzag around all edges, taking in the strip ends. Turn over 2 " of felt to form top and bottom flaps, iron along the folds and stitch down the flaps at each corner.

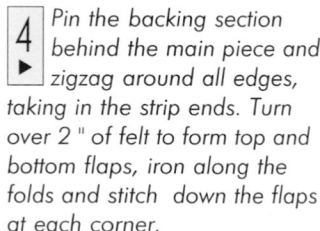

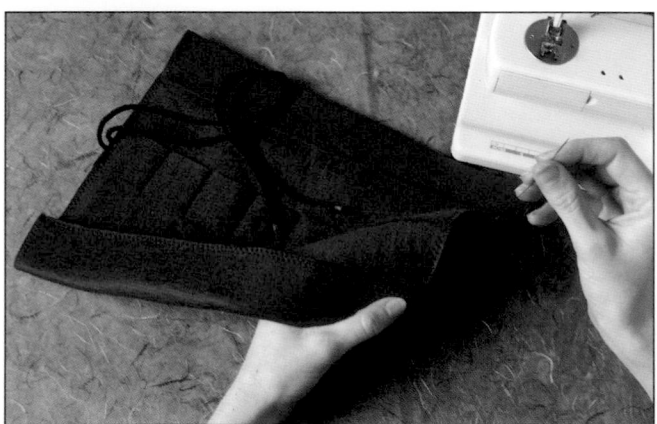

PROJECT 5

Cot String

YOU WILL NEED
colored felt
narrow ribbons
fiber filler
paper
a pencil
sewing equipment

These felt fish swim about charmingly when hung across a baby's cot or bassinet. Choose a color combination to suit the baby's room.

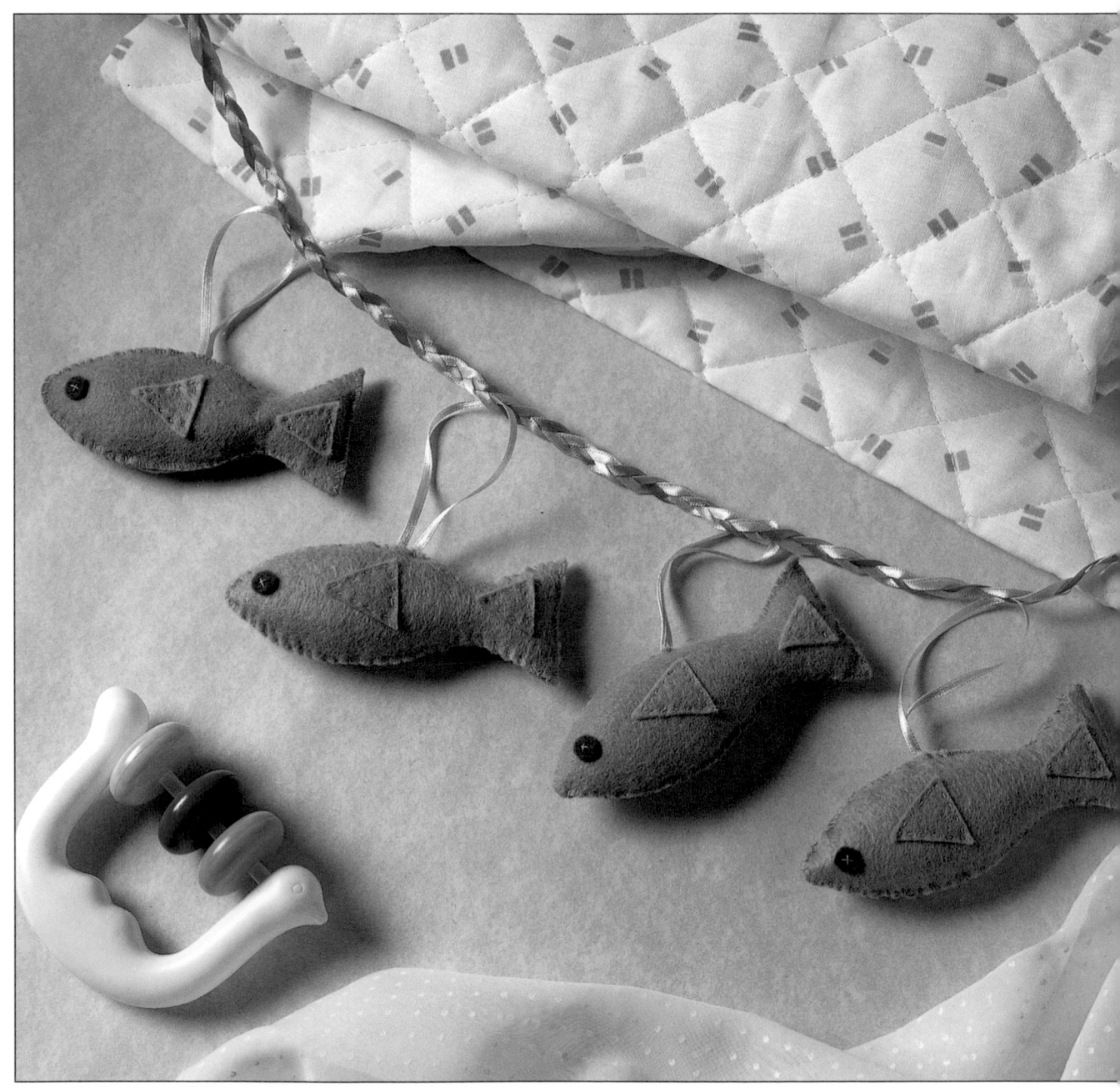

1 ▶ Trace the fish pattern onto paper and cut it out to make a template. Use the template to cut out pieces in felt: for each fish you will need two each of body, tail, fin, and eye. Handsew sets of small pieces onto differently colored bodies.

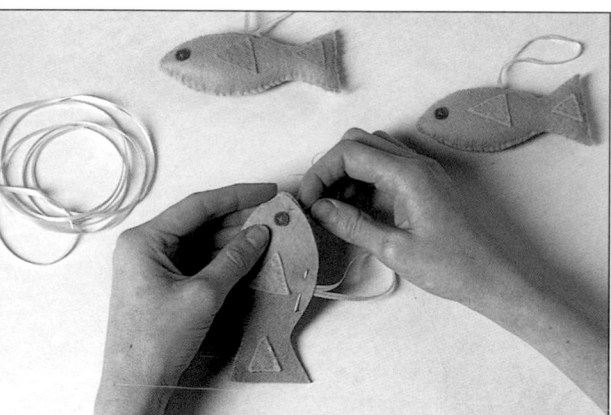

2 ◀ Place two decorated body sections together with wrong sides facing. Cut a loop of ribbon and pin the ends between the two body sections. Test by dangling the fish; if necessary, move the ribbon so that the fish hangs without tipping. Handsew around the fish, leaving a gap at the tail.

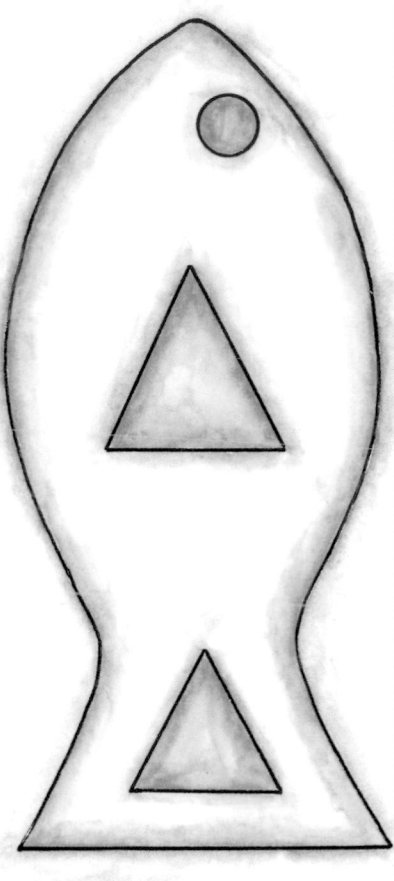

3 Gently poke a small amount of polyester fiber filler into the fish with a pencil, making sure that it is evenly filled. Sew the gap closed.

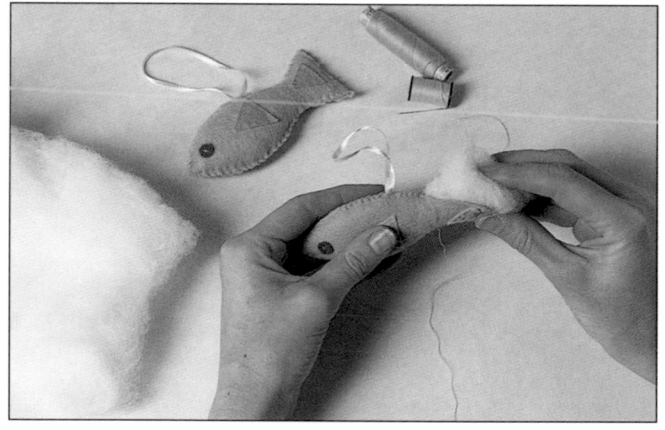

4 ◀ Knot three lengths of ribbon together, tape the knotted ends to a fixed surface and braid them. When you have braided a short distance, thread a fish onto one of the ribbons and continue braiding. Repeat this so that the fish are evenly spaced and the braid reaches across the cot. Knot the other end and trim.

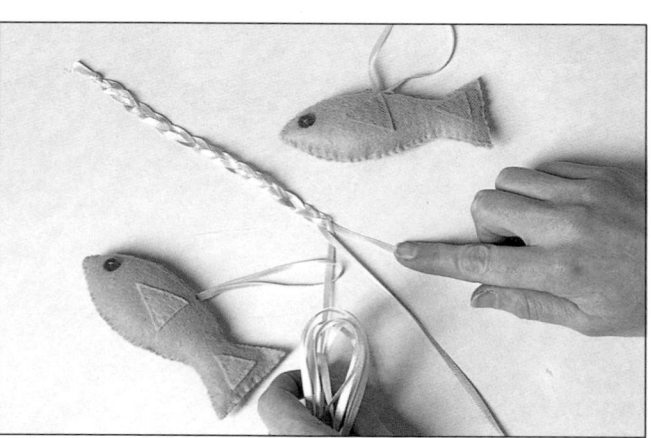

PROJECT 6

Winter Hat

YOU WILL NEED
- wool rolags
- nylon netting
- strong thread
- gold thread
- a tape measure
- a needle
- scissors
- buttons

Handmade felt gives a project a very natural look. When cutting the pieces for this hat, try to leave a raw edge along the edge of the cap.

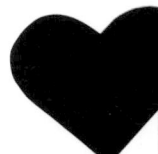

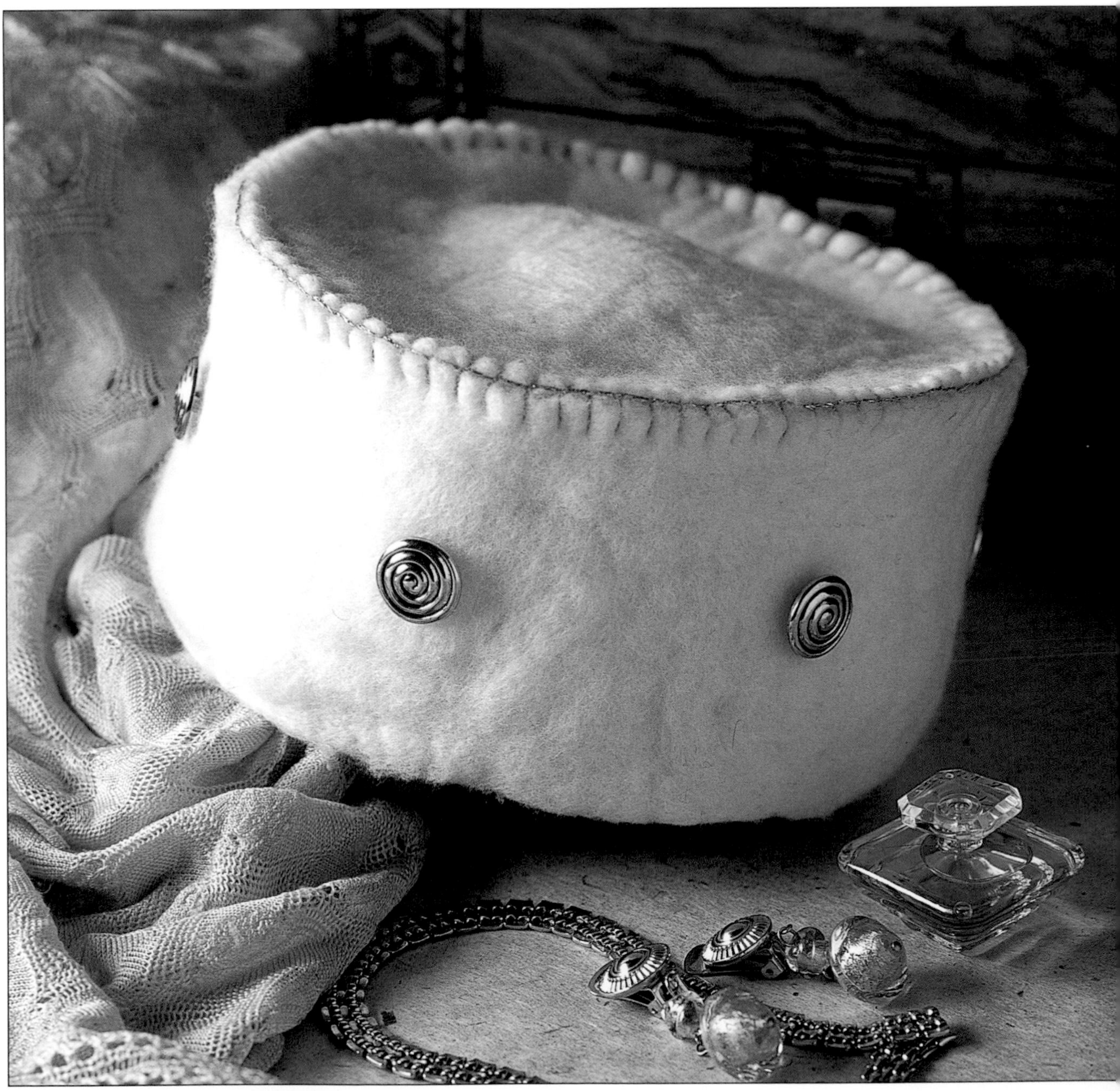

1 Make a piece of thick felt by following the instructions on page 25. For this project, you will need to make a piece 23 x 12 ", which will require approximately 4 oz of wool rolags (ie. rolls of wool).

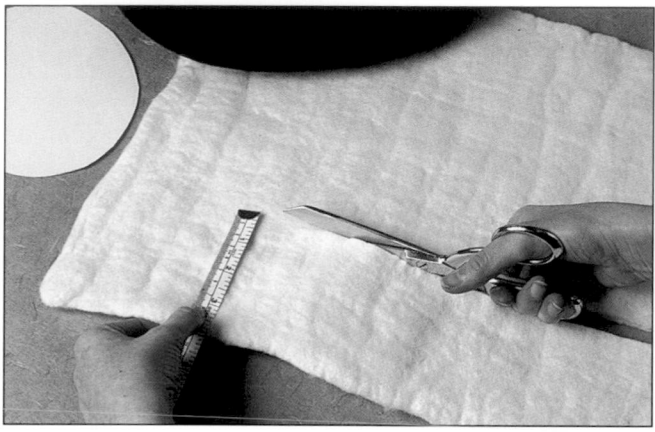

2 Measure around your head with a tape measure (or use a hat that fits as a guide) and cut a strip of felt this length and 3 " wide. From paper, cut an oval template with a perimeter that matches the felt strip. Use this template to cut a felt oval for the top of the hat.

3 Position a series of interesting buttons along the hat band at regular intervals and pin them in place. Stitch the buttons on securely. Overlap the two ends of the band by ½ " and slipstitch them together so that the stitches are not visible from the outside.

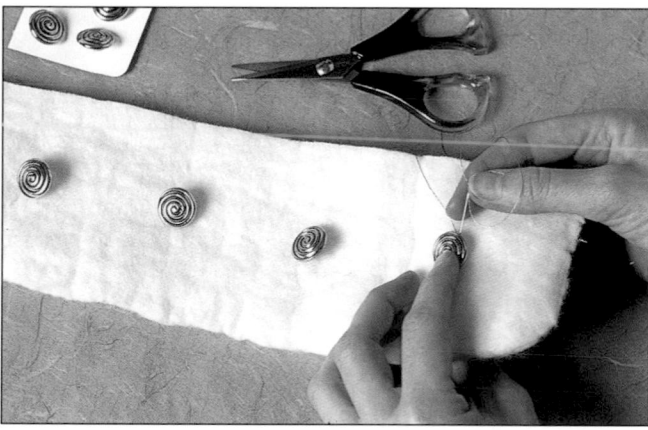

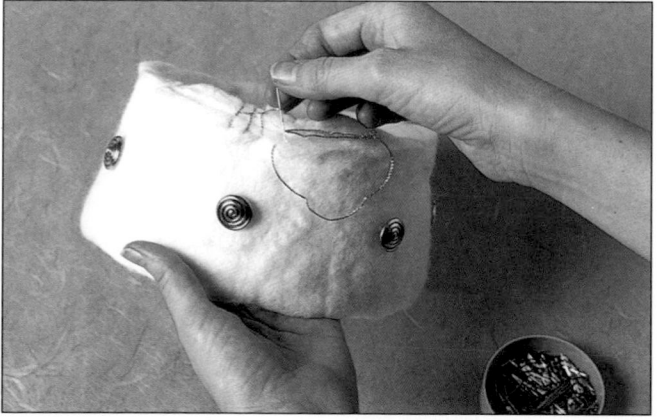

4 Pin the felt oval along the top of the band. Using strong gold thread, sew the two sections together with a blanket stitch. Working from left to right, bring the needle through the two layers to the side of the hat. Insert it through the top edge and bring it out on the side with the thread under the needle. Repeat this, decorating the edge.

Scrapcrafts

In these days of mass production and mass consumption, we have forgotten how precious a thing fabric once was. Fibers, dyes and woven cloth were important items in trade and world economy for centuries. To rural communities, especially pioneer ones, the planting and harvesting of flax or cotton crops, or the tending and shearing of sheep, were a only a precursor to treating, spinning and weaving the fibers into cloth.

Understandably, after so many months of labor, furnishings and clothing were treasured until they wore thin. When they could no longer serve their original purpose, they were patched into coverlets, reincarnated as dolls, or cut into long strips, dyed, and woven into rag rugs.

One of the most economical uses of small scraps was the crazy block method of constructing patchwork. Scraps of any shape and color, but of similar weight, are stitched onto a plain backing fabric, each piece overlapping slightly onto the surrounding ones. Embroidery is then worked where the patches overlap, covering the raw edges and preventing fraying. Herringbone, feather and cross stitch were all commonly used and, in the 19th century when this method became something of a craze itself, buttons, tokens, lace and ribbons were all sewn on for extra decoration. Project 8 draws on this idea, and you might like to add the patchwork to complete it.

Scraps can, of course, be used with any of the patchwork and appliqué techniques described in later chapters. It is delightful to be able to identify the source of fabric pieces in a quilt or other patched project, and it makes such pieces even more of a family heirloom. When you have finished making clothes, furnishings, or other large projects, sort the remaining scraps into colors or types of pattern: checks, florals, and so on, and put them in clear plastic bags so you can find them later.

If you don't have any scraps left over from earlier projects, check the remnants bin at fabric stores.

Bear essentials
You only need small pieces of fabric to make decorations such as this tiny bear. For a larger toy, sew together different scraps to create a patchwork bear.

Heart strings
For that country look, cut heart shapes and sew them roughly: irregular shapes will add to the appeal. Turn and fill the hearts then sew them closed and tie them together with raffia. Add a few cinnamon sticks to complete the effect.

Braided wreath
Cut strips in three contrasting fabrics, fold each lengthwise and sew a seam to form a long tube. Turn each one right side out and fill with fiber filler or sand. Braid the tubes and sew the ends together. Conceal these ends with a large bow of ribbon or fabric.

PROJECT 7

Braided Mat

YOU WILL NEED

*three fabrics
adhesive tape
sewing equipment*

*Braiding scraps of fabric into large floor mats was a popular
and cost-effective pastime in colonial America. Here the method
is used to create smaller mats for hot containers.*

1 ▶ Cut fabric into long strips 2 " wide. Fold each strip in half lengthwise. Overlap the folded ends of three strips in different colors to form a T shape. Fold the two side strips in half again, over the top of the vertical strip of material. Stitch the ends to secure the T shape.

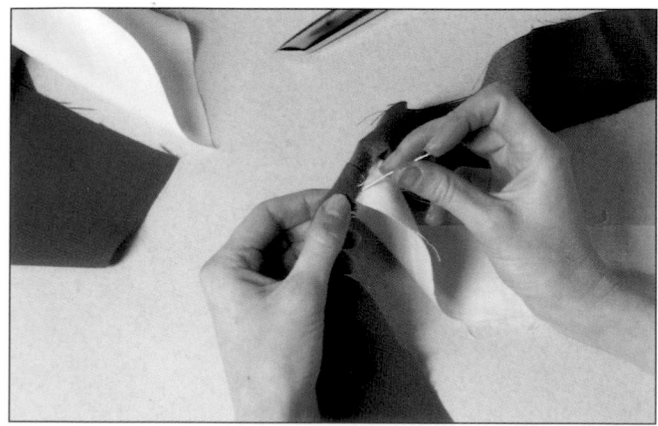

2 ◀ Tape the stitched T end to a fixed surface to give a good hold for braiding. Twist one side piece down and over the central strip. Repeat with the second side piece. Continue braiding evenly, bunching each strip loosely as you work so that the braid retains a slightly ragged appearance.

3 ◀ Coil the braid as you work to see how much braided material you are creating. When each strip of fabric is almost completely braided, sew an extra strip at the end and continue braid-ing. Work the braid until your coil reaches the required size, approximately 8 " in diameter.

4 ▶ Finish off by flattening the end and stitching it underneath the coil. Pin the completed braid into a coil. You may need to stretch and twist the braid to flatten it as you work. On the least attractive side, sew the edges of the braids to secure the coiled shape.

PROJECT 8

Crazy Vest

YOU WILL NEED

vest pattern
fabric
lining fabric
lace
buttons
beads
a sewing machine
sewing equipment

Here is an attractive way to make use of those odd buttons, beads and short scraps of lace. The same concept can also be worked on a cushion or padded box.

1 ◄ Choose a commercial pattern for a vest. Cut out the fabric and lining and staystitch them according to the pattern's instructions. Arrange strips of lace on the front panels and pin them, making sure the two panels are complementary.

2 ◄ Machine sew the lace in position. Iron the panels and handle them carefully from this point, so as not to crease the vest. Handsew a variety of beads and buttons in an attractive arrangement.

3 ► With the right sides of the fabric facing each other, sew the front panels and the back of the vest together at the shoulders. Likewise, sew the pieces of the lining together.

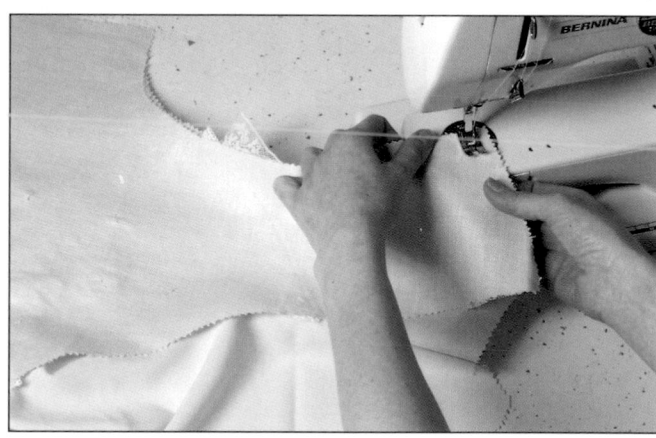

4 ► Pin and sew the outer vest to the lining according to the pattern's instructions. Finish off as per the pattern.

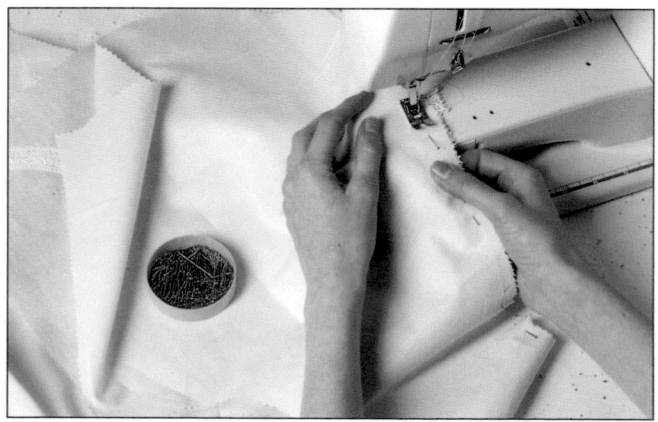

PROJECT 9

Rag Dolls

Scraps of muslin and country ginghams are the main ingredients for these rustic rag dolls, sure to win hearts wherever they go.

YOU WILL NEED
muslin
patterned scraps
wool scraps
fiber filler
paper
a pencil
ribbon
sewing equipment
a sewing machine

1 ◄ *Enlarge the doll pattern on page 158 by 200% (see page 14). Cut out two muslin pieces to this shape. Lay them together and sew a ½ " seam around all the edges, leaving a gap between the legs for turning. Snip into the seam at sharp curves. Turn right side out, and push in fiber filler.*

2 ► *Turn in the edges at the gap and slipstitch it closed. Machine across the doll's hips: this will let it bend better for sitting. To sew each eye, bring a threaded needle through from the back of the head, sew a cross stitch, and tie it off at the back tightly. Stitch scraps of wool to the top of the head for hair.*

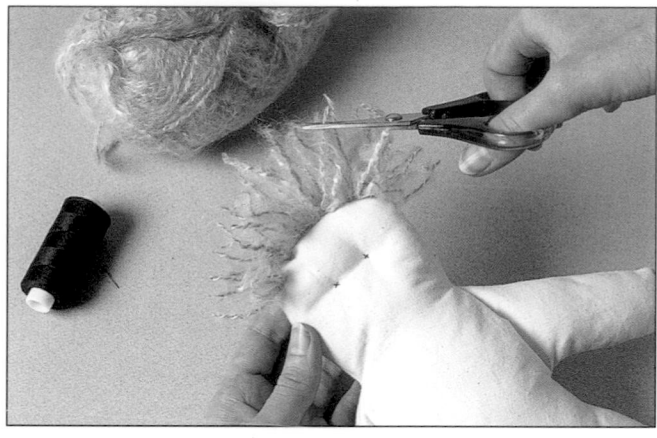

3 ► *Enlarge the dress pattern on page 158 by 200% and cut two pieces from patterned fabric. Staystitch them, then lay them together, right sides facing, and sew a ¼ " seam across the shoulders and down the sides. Turn and sew a ¾ " hem at the base and armholes. Turn the dress right side out. Dress the doll, then tie a ribbon at the waist.*

4 ► *For the shawl, cut a triangle with two sides of 12 " and one of 16 ". Sew a ¼ " hem around all edges. For the headscarf, cut a 16 x 6 " band. Fold it in half, right sides together, and cut a curve along one long edge. Sew a ¼ " seam along the curve, leaving a gap for turning.*

Canvaswork

The working of embroidered designs on canvas has a long tradition which began as a means of imitating the richness of woven tapestries; some people still refer to canvaswork as "tapestry."

The craft developed over time as materials changed: in the Middle Ages counted stitches were mixed with free embroidery on a coarse linen cloth. During the 17th and 18th centuries, a number of counted stitches were created and sections of a design were worked in the same stitch. Many of these stitches bear the names of the towns where they originated, such as Gobelin and Aubusson. Tent stitch, from the French *tenter* "to stretch" (referring to the technique of stretching the background fabric on a frame) was used for such things as book covers, bags and pin cushions.

In the 19th century, Germany produced printed paper designs, along with brightly dyed wools and stiff canvas, making "Berlin woolwork" an immensely popular pastime. Footstools, bellpulls, firescreens, and any number of household items were worked by the Victorians.

Today, canvaswork or needlepoint is a well-established craft in which counted stitches are worked on an evenly woven mesh so as to cover the canvas, an aspect that distinguishes it from counted cross stitch. Printed canvases are available, but you can also transfer a design from a chart onto blank canvas by calculating the number and shape of stitches in each color. There are many books of such charted designs and, after stitching several of these, you may well prefer to design your own.

A frame, while not essential, keeps the canvas evenly stretched and frees both your hands for stitching.

ent stitch
A diagonal stitch
over one cross-band
of mesh, worked in
straight rows.

Florentine stitch
A straight stitch over a
specified number of
mesh bands, worked in
zigzag patterns.

Your choice of thread type
depends on the purpose of the
project and the size of the canvas.
The threads should cover the
canvas, so fine threads such as
cotton or crewel wool may need
to be used in multiple strands.

If the finished work is
distorted, it should be
stretched back into
shape. Pin it on a piece of
cardboard or polystyrene
so that it is square. Spray
it with water and leave it
to dry.

Canvas mesh size can
range from 10 to 32
bands per inch. A
14-count canvas
has 14 bands per 1 ".
Canvas is woven in
either single or
double bands.

Tapestry needles have a round point
and an elongated eye, suitable for
threading wool. Choose a needle
slightly thicker than your thread and
finer than the canvas holes.

PROJECT 10

Glasses Case

YOU WILL NEED
14-count canvas
embroidery yarn
a tapestry needle
lining fabric
a small frame
masking tape
sewing equipment

This attractive case for spectacles or sunglasses is decorated
with Scottish stitch, so called because it looks a little like tartan.
Choose a color scheme to suit your own taste.

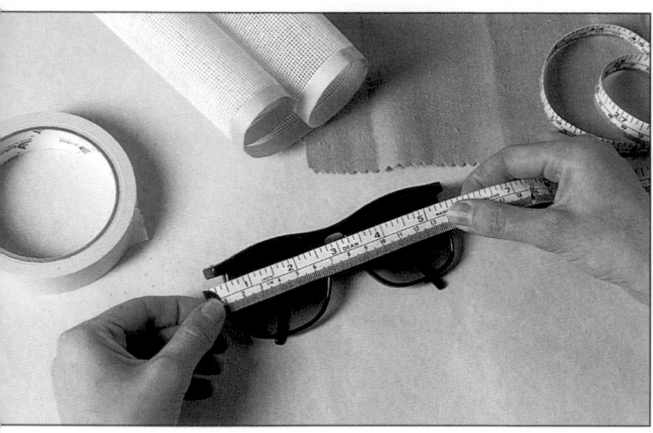

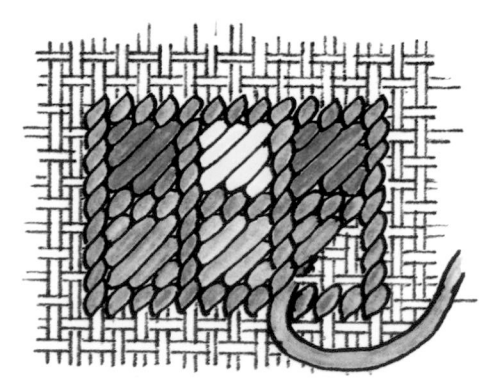

1 Measure the glasses and calculate the size of case required. Cut a long piece of 14-count canvas that can be folded in half to form the case, and allow 2" around the pattern area. Tape the edges and secure it onto a small frame if one is available.

2 Stitch the design according to the pattern. The brown grid is a series of tent stitches (see page 41) and the colored squares are each made up of five diagonal stitches of varying lengths. When you jump from one colored square to the next, secure the yarn at the back under a few existing stitches.

3 When complete, stretch the canvaswork as shown on page 41 if necessary. Trim the canvas to ½" around the design and fold the edges over. Fold the canvas in half, with wrong sides facing and the seam allowance tucked inside. Slipstitch along the two sides, starting each time at the fold and working towards the opening.

4 Cut a matching piece of lining fabric and fold it in half with right sides facing. Sew a seam along the two sides to create a narrow bag. Push the fabric bag, wrong side out, into the canvas one. Turn the edges of both bags in at the mouth of the case and neatly handsew the lining to the canvas.

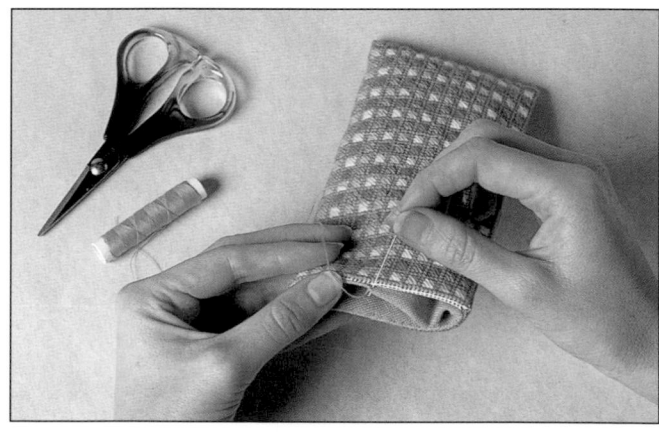

PROJECT 11

Soft Toy

YOU WILL NEED
12-count canvas
tapestry wools
a frame
backing fabric
fiber filler
sewing equipment

This cheerful fellow is worked in simple tent stitch by following the chart. He is sure to bring a smile to any small child's face.

1 ◀ Cut a 10 x 8 " piece of 12-count canvas and secure it on a frame. Work the design in tent stitch (see page 41), referring to the key for colors in the DMC range of tapestry wools. Half the pattern is given; reverse the chart to work the other side.

KEY	
Symbol	DMC No.
+	7104
▼	7243
—	7598
○	7709
×	7853
•	white

2 ▲ If the finished work is distorted, stretch it back into shape (see page 41). Trim the canvas ½ " from the stitching. Cut a matching piece of backing fabric and staystitch around it. Lay the two sections together, right sides facing, and sew around the tent stitches, leaving a gap for turning.

3 ▼ Turn the clown right side out. Push fiber filler into the opening and ensure the toy is evenly filled before handsewing the gap closed.

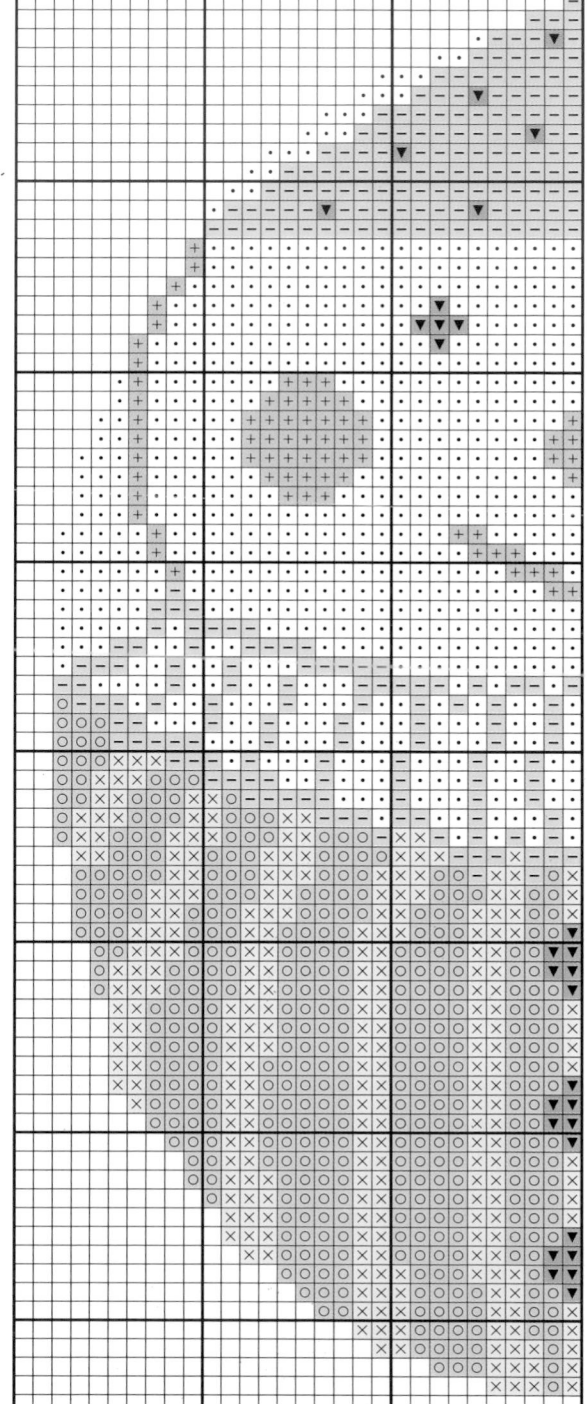

Cushion

This flame pattern is characteristic of Florentine stitch, a type of bargello. The cushion can be made to whatever dimensions you like, but plan to end at a suitable point in the flame design.

YOU WILL NEED
11-count canvas
tapestry wools
pearl cotton
backing fabric
fiber filler
a frame
a tapestry needle
piping cord
sewing equipment
a sewing machine

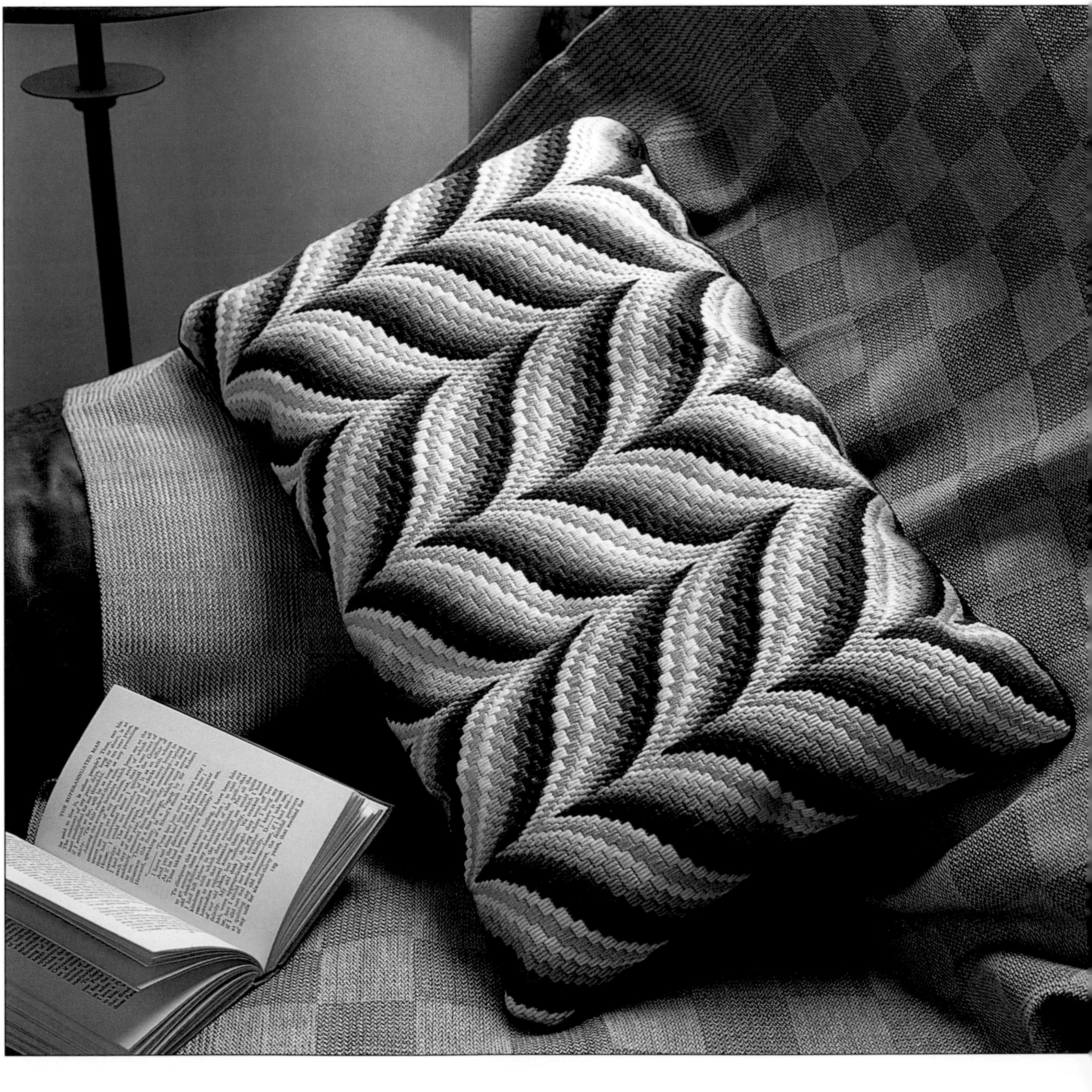

1 Secure a large piece of 11-count canvas onto a frame. Work the design in florentine stitch (see page 41). Each stitch covers four bands of the canvas. Stitch colors in waves. The colors used in the cushion pictured are 7329, 7327, 7326, 7323, 7322, white (all DMC tapestry wools) and 353 (DMC pearl cotton).

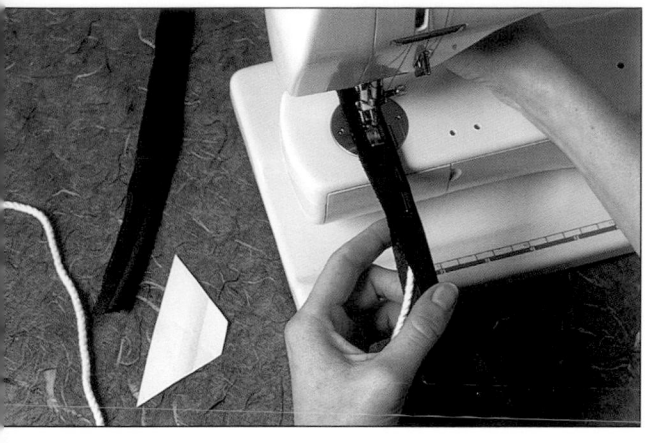

2 From the backing fabric, cut 1¼ " wide strips on the diagonal. Sew these together to form a long strip which will fit around your stitched canvas. Lay piping cord along the center of the wrong side of this bias strip, fold the strip over and secure with pins. Use the zipper foot to machine along the strip, encasing the cord.

3 Trim the canvas to within ½ " of the stitched design and lay it right side up. Pin the covered piping around the stitched area, so that the raw edges of the bias are aligned to the raw edges of the canvas. Curve the piping gently at the corners. Baste the piping to the canvas.

4 Staystitch a piece of backing fabric to match the canvas. Lay the two together, right sides facing, with the piping between them, and pin the layers. Sew a seam around three sides of the cushion, staying on the outside of the piping. Turn the cushion right side out, fill with fiber and handsew the fourth side closed.

Ribbon & Lace

A snippet of ribbon and a scrap of lace can change a project from something plain and practical into a special gift with an air of indulgence. They can add a romantic touch, and are particularly suitable for pillowslips, guest towels and items in the nursery.

Ribbon can be bought in an amazing array of colors, widths and textures. Ribbon with a satin finish is much more attractive than the matte type and not much more expensive. Wire-edged ribbons do cost a bit more, but they are wonderful to shape and have a long life if handled carefully. They are ideal for use in wreaths, swags and other large arrangements. Narrow satin ribbon can even be used for embroidery, reproducing flowers and leaves beautifully.

If you do lots of craftwork, it is very helpful to have a selection of ribbons on hand, saving you a special trip to the store. A collection can easily become tangled, so store them on spools or wound around old cardboard tubes.

Lace became a fashion accessory during the Renaissance. The French court took the fashion to extremes with lace frills decorating cuffs, collars and knee britches. During this period, and indeed up until this century, lace was hand woven in silk or cotton threads using carved bobbins. With the introduction of mechanization and synthetic threads, lace became less of a luxury.

Cotton lace is still readily available and is much nicer to use than the nylon sort, especially if you are working with natural fabrics. Lace comes in many forms such as tape and edgings. Lace insertion is a type of lace which can be used to join two pieces of fabric: some examples have slits for threading ribbons through. Store lace in a dark, dry place and keep it rolled rather than folded.

Guest towels
A snatch of lace and
a snip of ribbon turn a
plain cloth or towel into
something special.
Eyelet embroidery and
ribbon embroidery
decorate the white
cloth. The cream towel
is edged with insertion
lace.

Tissue sachet
Pin a lace trim on each end of a
piece of fabric. Place lining on top,
sew the laced edges and turn. Fold
the laced edges in to the center
and sew a seam along the other
sides. Turn the sachet out and
insert a packet of paper tissues.

Perfect bows
Wire-edged ribbon holds
the shape you want and
is ideal for lavish bows.

Ribbon roses
Ribbon can be rolled
and twisted to make
pretty rosebuds for
decorating hats or gifts.

PROJECT 13

Clothes hangers

YOU WILL NEED
wooden clothes hanger
thick wadding
eyelet embroidery
cotton fabric
narrow ribbon
double-sided tape
sewing equipment

Apart from adding a romantic touch to a wardrobe, these padded clothes hangers protect the shoulders of good clothing. They make a quick but charming gift.

1 ▶ Cut narrow strips of double-sided tape and lay them along the back of a narrow ribbon. Wind the ribbon tightly around the hook of the clothes hanger, spiraling as you work, to cover it neatly. Secure the end in place with a few stitches.

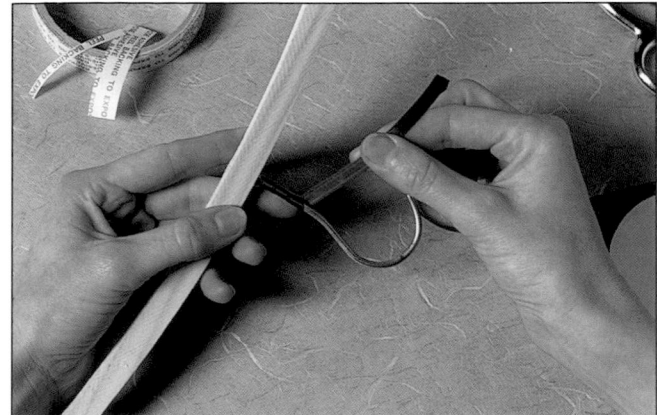

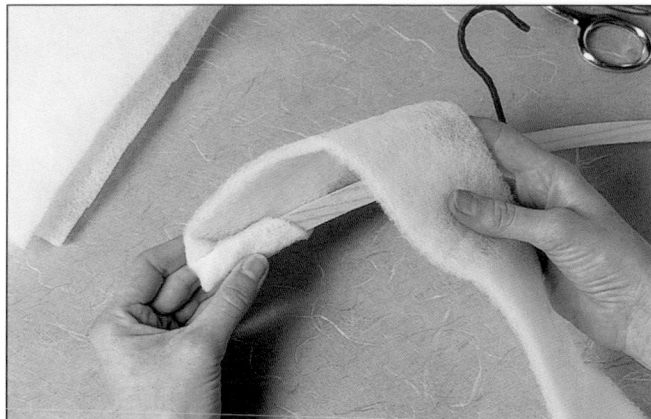

2 ◀ Cut a strip of polyester wadding 4 x 40 " wide. Fold one end around the end of the clothes hanger as shown. Wind the wadding strip around the clothes hanger, folding the other end over and securing it with a few stitches.

3 ▶ With pinking shears, cut a piece of cotton fabric 4 " wide and 1½ " longer than your clothes hanger. Fold and iron a seam all around. Lay the wadded clothes hanger in the center and fold the cotton fabric to cover it. Handsew the folded edges of the cotton together.

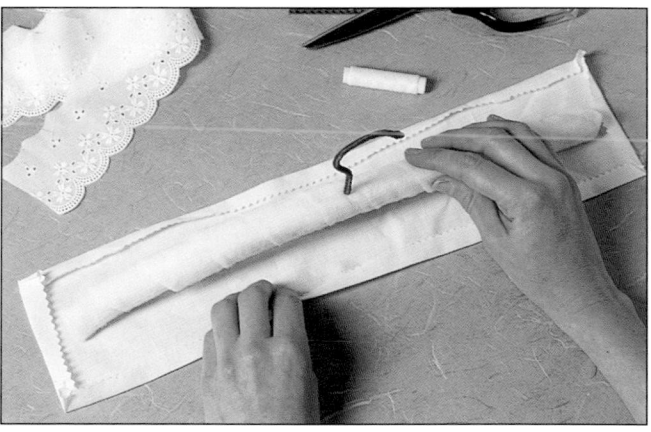

4 ▶ Cut a length of eyelet embroidery twice as long as the clothes hanger plus a seam allowance. Fold in half, right sides facing, and mark where the hook will be. Sew a seam along the raw edge, leaving a gap for the hook and curving down at each end. Turn the cover right side out and slip it over the hook. Add a ribbon bow.

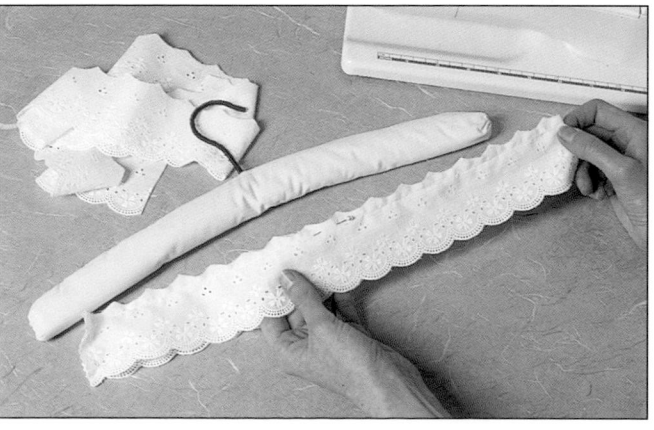

PROJECT 14

Rosettes

YOU WILL NEED
satin ribbons
matching fabrics
large safety pins
a pencil
a compass
sewing equipment

For a special treat, you could make one of these for each child at a party and award them after games. The letters add a personal touch.

1 Mark a letter approximately ¾ " high onto fabric with tailor's chalk. Set the sewing machine to a tight zigzag pattern and sew along the marked letter, sewing over it twice for a darker color. Draw a circle with a 1 " radius around the letter and cut it out with pinking shears.

2 Draw another circle with a 1⅛ " radius and cut this out with pinking shears. Handsew a length of satin ribbon around the perimeter of this, gathering it as you sew to create a ruffled edge. Cut the ends of the ribbon at an angle and overlap them.

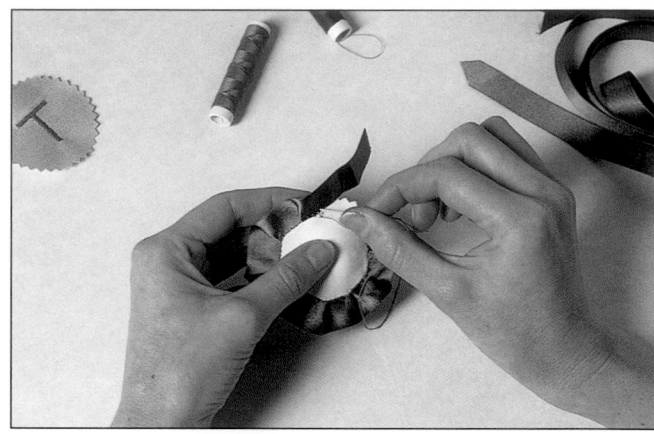

3 Cut two tags of ribbon and position them over the raw ends of the ruffle. Lay the embroidered letter on top and sew around the letter, stitching the layers together.

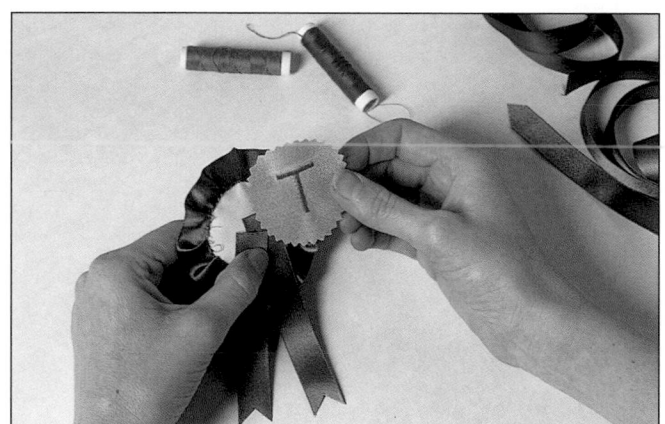

4 On the back of the rosette, sew down one bar of a large safety pin, securing the wire loop at the base so that the pin doesn't slip around.

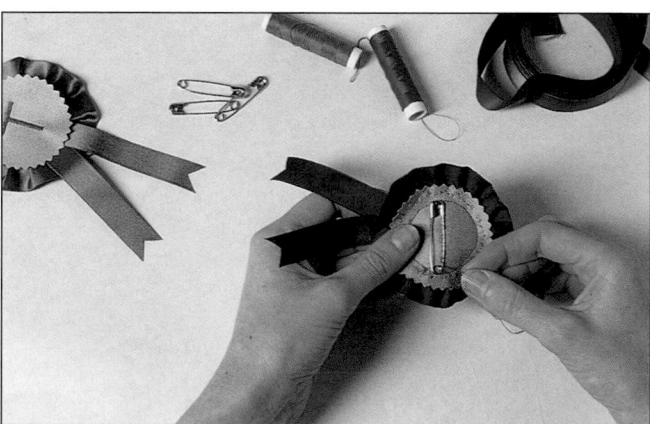

PROJECT 15

Cot Linen

YOU WILL NEED
fine cotton
insertion lace
ribbons
sewing equipment
a sewing machine

A set of cot linen makes a thoughtful gift to mark the arrival of a new baby. It takes only a short while to add a special touch with ribbons and lace.

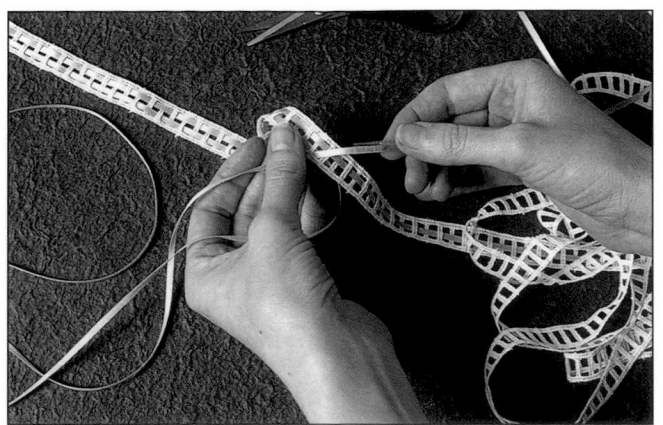

1 ◄ Cut a piece of fine white cotton to suit your cot size. Sew narrow seams along the sides and base of the sheet, and a generous seam along the top. Cut a piece of insertion lace slightly longer than the top of the sheet and lace two narrow ribbons through alternating holes, as shown.

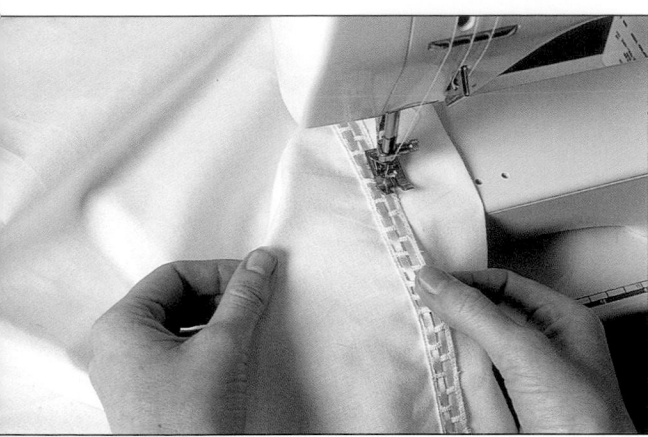

2 ◄ On the right side of the sheet, position the lace along the top so that it conceals the seam. Pin it in place, making sure that the ribbons are lying flat. Machine sew along both sides of the lace. Neatly stitch down the ends of the ribbons and the lace at either side on the back of the sheet.

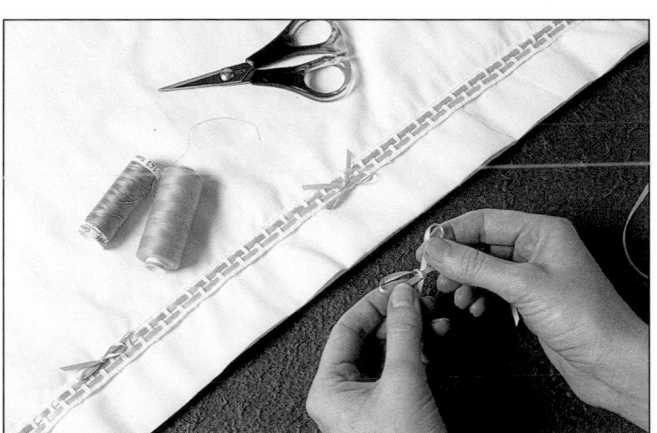

3 ◄ Tie small bows in each color of ribbon and position them along the lace at regular intervals. Secure each one in place with a few stitches using strong thread so they cannot easily be pulled off.

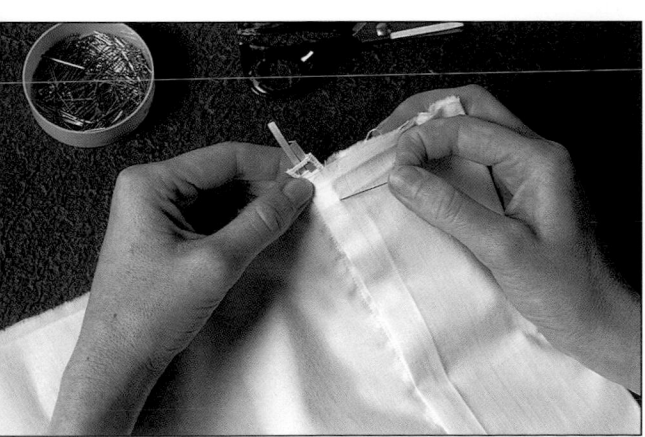

4 ◄ To make a matching pillow case, measure a nursery pillow and cut fabric twice the size with an allowance for a fold at one end and a seam allowance all around. Sew a length of ribboned lace onto the fabric before sewing the pillow together.

Patchwork

Also known as "piecing," patchwork is the technique of sewing small pieces of fabric together to form a large piece. Many choose to make this large piece into a bed quilt or wall hanging, but it can equally be turned into a bag, a jacket, or a case for your spectacles. The projects in this chapter offer a few other ideas.

The pieces for patchwork can be regular shapes, such as diamonds, clamshells, or octagons, or they can be irregularly shaped. "Crazy" patchwork is made with scraps of any shape, embroidered along the edges.

The use of blocks, repeated units of shapes such as squares and triangles, started in Europe, but it was developed by American colonials, who turned it into an art form. Particular arrangements of shapes were identified by names, many of which were drawn from religious themes or national events. These blocks could be worked one at a time and then stitched together. In settle-

ments where work space was limited, communities of women would gather together for the final stage of piecing together blocks so that a quilt could be completed quickly. For this reason, patchwork and the making of quilts has long been associated with friendship and community spirit.

The patterns possible with the block method are unlimited. Individual blocks can be set apart by sashing, long strips of plain fabric. This design is used in album quilts, where each block has a different construction. Juxtaposing blocks without sashing can create a secondary, more complex pattern.

The piecing together of blocks can be done by hand, but a sewing machine speeds up the process enormously without any loss of quality. One method which does require handsewing is paper patchwork, an example of which is given in Project 18. This technique, using paper templates in a uniform shape, requires some precision and is ideal for smaller projects. It is also portable, an advantage for those who like to patchwork away from the sewing room.

A rotary cutter and clear grid will speed up the cutting out process a great deal.

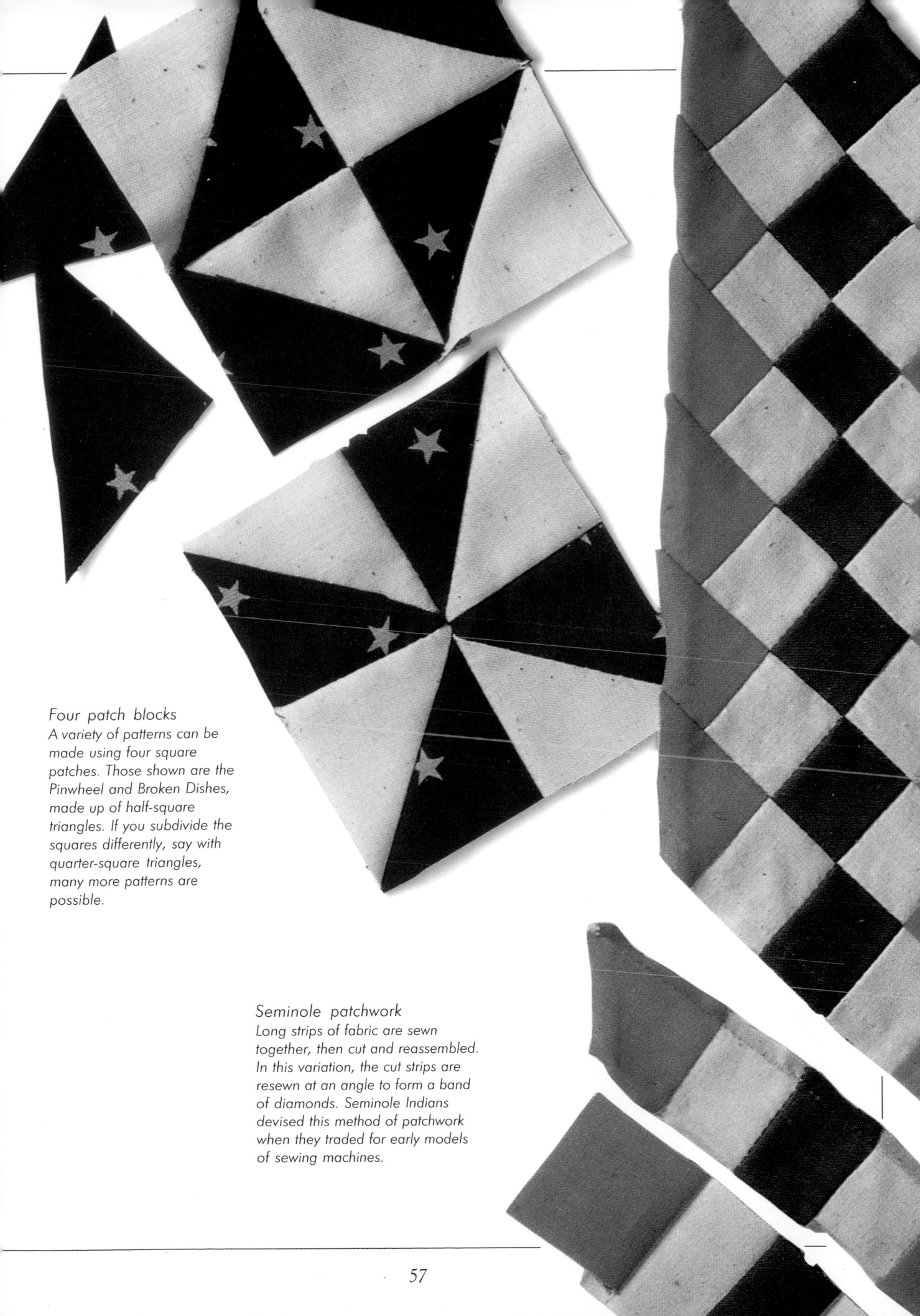

Four patch blocks
A variety of patterns can be
made using four square
patches. Those shown are the
Pinwheel and Broken Dishes,
made up of half-square
triangles. If you subdivide the
squares differently, say with
quarter-square triangles,
many more patterns are
possible.

Seminole patchwork
Long strips of fabric are sewn
together, then cut and reassembled.
In this variation, the cut strips are
resewn at an angle to form a band
of diamonds. Seminole Indians
devised this method of patchwork
when they traded for early models
of sewing machines.

PROJECT 16

Pin Cushion

YOU WILL NEED
colored fabrics
narrow piping cord
fiber filler
a compass or saucer
tailor's chalk
sewing equipment
a sewing machine

*Everyone who sews needs a pin cushion and here's
a good opportunity to try out your patchwork technique
while using up small scraps of fabric.*

1 ▶ Cut strips of colored fabric 1½ " wide and 6 " long. Lay two strips together with right sides facing and sew a ¼ " seam. Repeat with the next strip until you have a square piece of patchwork. Iron the seams flat.

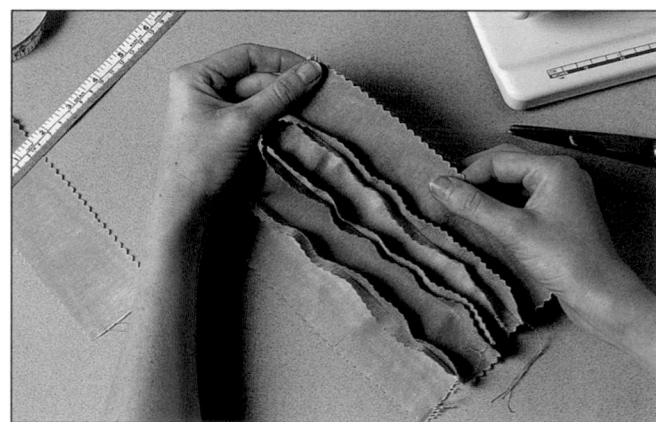

2 ◀ Use a compass or a small dish to mark and cut a circle with a diameter of 5½ " for the top. Cut a matching circle for the base, either from plain fabric or from another patched piece. Cut a plain 3 x 16 " piece for the side. Cut a piece 1 x 16 " along the diagonal of the fabric as a bias strip.

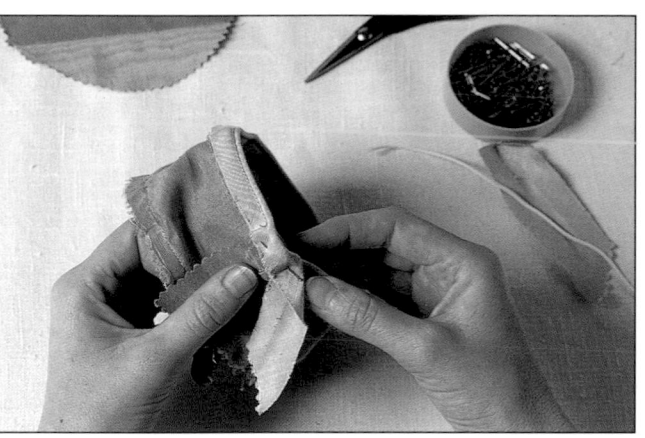

3 ◀ Lay a piece of narrow piping cord along the wrong side of the bias strip, fold the strip over and secure with pins. Use the zipper foot on the sewing machine to stitch along the cord. Lay the side piece right side up and pin the covered piping along one edge with the raw edges of the bias aligned. Sew in position.

4 ▶ Pin the side and base together, right sides facing, and sew a ½ " seam. Sew the ends of the side strip. Trim the cord, fold one end of the bias strip under and stitch it so that it neatly overlaps the other end. Turn the pin cushion right side out and fill it with fiber. Pin the top section in place and slipstitch it onto the piping.

Suggestion: The ideal filler for pin cushions is untreated sheep's wool, as the natural grease prevents the pins from rusting.

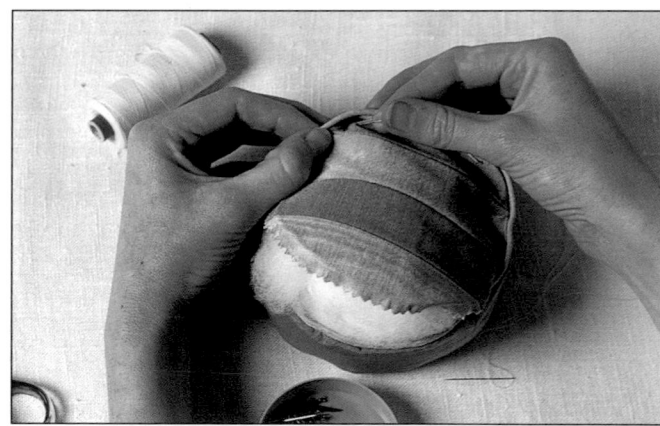

PROJECT 17

Juggling Toys

YOU WILL NEED
satin fabric
seeds or beans
paper
sewing equipment
a sewing machine

*These exquisite juggling sacks have a curious design which
makes them beautiful to look at and a delight to use.
No matter if you can't juggle—now's the time to learn!*

1 Cut a paper rectangle measuring 2³/₈ x 4 ". Use this template to cut four rectangles from each of three colors, giving you twelve rectangles to make three juggling sacks. Staystitch around the edges.

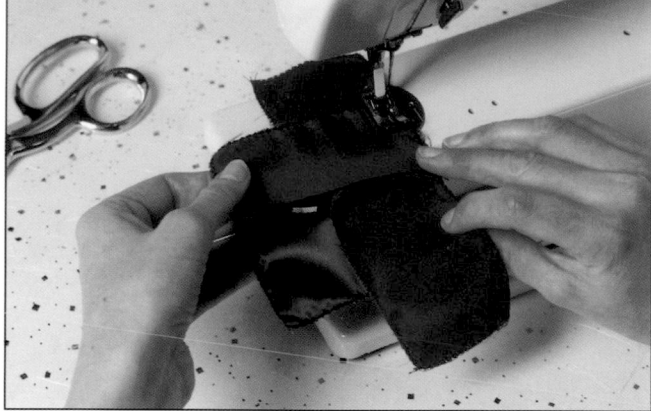

2 Lay two contrasting sections together, right sides facing. The short end of the top section should lie along the side of the other. Sew a ³/₈ " seam, starting and ending ³/₈ " from the edges of the top section. Flatten the seam. Repeat this with another pair in the same two colors.

3 Lay the two double sections together with seams aligned and right sides facing: the short ends of one color should lie along the sides of the other. Sew a ³/₈ " seam, starting and ending ³/₈ " from the edges of the top section. When you unfold the sewn piece, it should form a windmill shape.

4 With the wrong side facing you, bend one flap over and pin its side to the side of the adjoining flap. Sew a ³/₈ " seam as above. Work around the windmill in this way, sewing sides to sides so that it becomes three-dimensional. Continue until two seams remain unsewn.

5 Turn the sack right side out and fill it with seeds, rice or small beans. Do not overfill: the filling should be loose. Turn the raw edges in and pin the two remaining seams. Handsew the seams, sealing the opening.

PROJECT 18

Tea Cozy

The English method of piecing together patches is used here to make a charming tea cozy. There are faster techniques but this one is both accurate and rewarding.

YOU WILL NEED
colored fabrics
lining fabric
stiff cardboard
scrap paper
a pencil
bias binding
piping cord
wadding
sewing equipment
a sewing machine

1 Transfer the two hexagons onto stiff cardboard and cut templates. Using the large hexagon, cut 60 fabric pieces. Using the small one, cut 60 papers. Lay a paper on the wrong side of a fabric hexagon, turn over the edges and tack, securing the fabric and paper together. Press.

Suggestion: If you have access to a photocopier, copy a sheet of small hexagons and then cut your 60 papers.

2 Measure your teapot and sketch a generous cozy shape with seam allowance. Lay two covered hexagons together, right sides facing. Join them along one edge with tiny overcasting stitches, avoiding piercing the papers. Attach another hexagon, and another, until you have two pieces larger than your cozy pattern.

3 Lay cord along the wrong side of bias binding. Fold the binding over and tack. Cover enough cord to decorate the curved edge of your cozy pattern. Cut 4 " of cord and cover it with bias binding, handsewing the edges to form the handle. Undo the tacking and remove the papers from the patch-work sections.

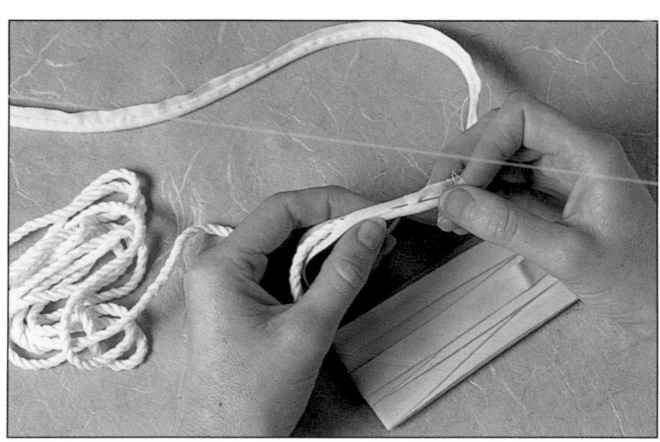

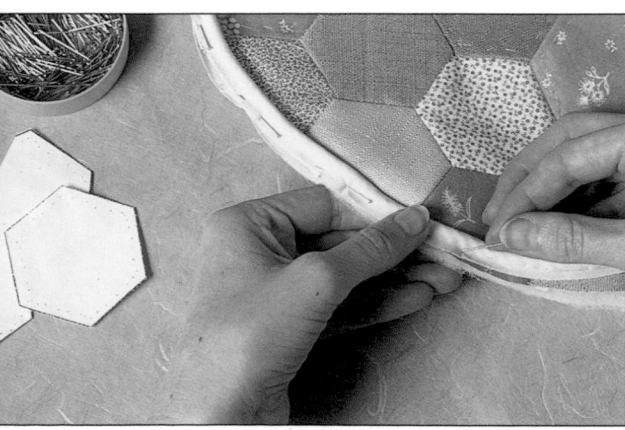

4 Cut patchwork, lining and wadding for each side of the cozy. Lay a patchwork piece face down on lining and sew along the base. Turn and insert wadding, then tack around the curve. Repeat this for the other side, securing the piping as shown. Lay the two side sections together, right sides facing, with the handle positioned between, and sew around the curve. Turn the cozy out.

Appliqué

Appliqué is the art of fabric collage: the process of stitching pieces of fabric onto a base material to create a pattern or design. This method of working with fabric affords the craftsperson more flexibility than patchwork does, as the pieces can be whatever shape you choose. Once you've learned the basics, you can let your imagination have free rein and create personalized pieces.

While appliqué is often used in combination with quilting to produce bedspreads, any project which shows the appliqué off to good effect is worth considering. Ancient nomadic tribes in Asia embellished their tents with this technique. Cushions, curtains, and picnic mats are just some ideas to inspire you.

Your choice of top fabric for appliquéing affects the technique you use. Felt, which doesn't fray, can simply be glued on and the edges left raw. With most fabrics, however, you will need to turn the edges under before stitching pieces in place, especially if the project will require regular washing. In this case, you will need to cut the pieces with a small seam allowance. Fabrics made from natural fibers—cotton, silk, fine wool—are best as they can be easily creased and folded at the edges. The backing fabric should be at least as heavy as the appliqué pieces. This is particularly important if the project is to be hung up, as heavy appliquéd pieces will hang badly on a sheer fabric.

Appliqué shapes can be tacked in place on the base fabric with long stitches, or attached with fusible webbing and a hot iron. The pieces can then be secured with slipstitching, which is almost invisible, or with decorative stitches. Alternatively, you can use the sewing machine to secure pieces with raw edges. This creates quite different possibilities, as the tight zigzag stitch can be used to add a decorative element or to add details.

A quite different approach to appliqué is taken by the Cuna Indians who live off the coast of Panama. They tack several layers of fabric together and then cut away sections to reveal the different colors below. This technique is known as reverse appliqué.

Fusible webbing or interfacing can be used to make the process of appliqué much easier.

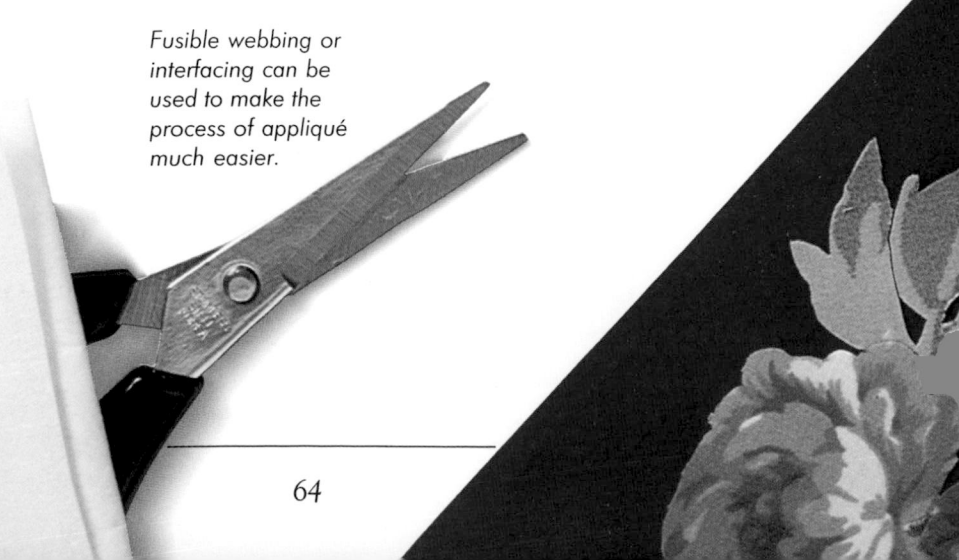

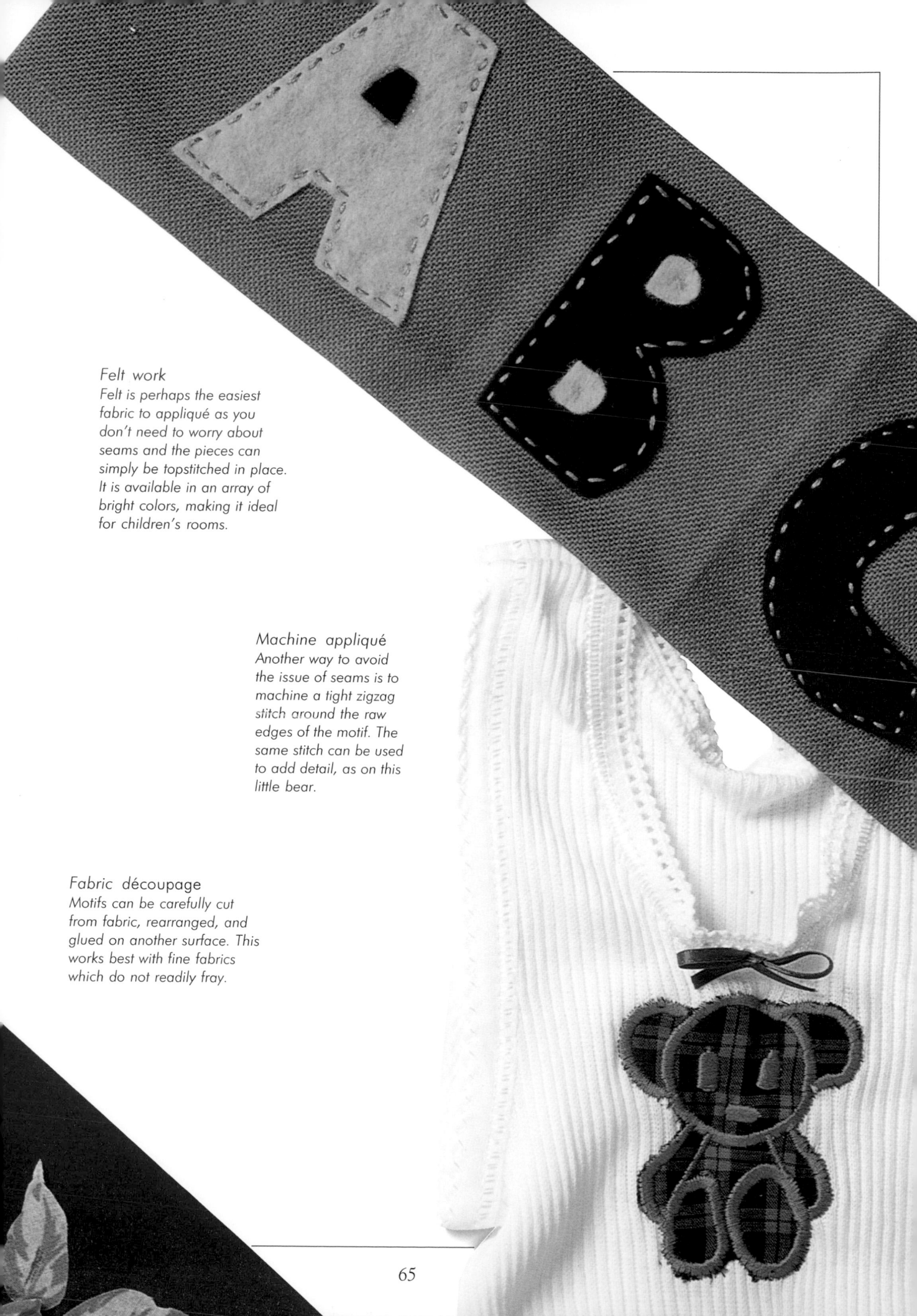

Felt work
Felt is perhaps the easiest fabric to appliqué as you don't need to worry about seams and the pieces can simply be topstitched in place. It is available in an array of bright colors, making it ideal for children's rooms.

Machine appliqué
Another way to avoid the issue of seams is to machine a tight zigzag stitch around the raw edges of the motif. The same stitch can be used to add detail, as on this little bear.

Fabric découpage
Motifs can be carefully cut from fabric, rearranged, and glued on another surface. This works best with fine fabrics which do not readily fray.

PROJECT 19

Pencil Case

Classic fleur-de-lis motifs embellish this attractive pencil case. It could also be used for cosmetics or for your sewing kit when traveling.

YOU WILL NEED
black fabric
lining fabric
colored fabrics
gold thread
a zipper
tracing paper
a pencil
fusible webbing
an iron
sewing equipment

1 Lay a piece of tracing paper over the patterns and draw over them with pencil. Lay this tracing face down on a sheet of paper-covered fusible webbing and pencil over the lines so the motif is transferred onto the paper. Iron the webbing onto the back of the colored fabric, following the instructions given. Cut out two large and four small motifs.

2 Cut a 10 x 11 " piece of black fabric and staystitch it. Fold it in half to form a 10 x 5½ " rectangle. Peel the backing paper off the motifs and arrange them on the fabric. Fuse them in place with a hot iron. Handstitch around each motif with bold, even stitches in gold thread.

3 Lay a 9 " black zip along one edge of the black fabric, right sides facing, and sew one side of the zip in place using a zipper foot. Fold the fabric in half, right sides facing, and sew the other side of the zip in place. With the zip open, sew a ½ " seam down each side. Trim the corners and turn the case right side out.

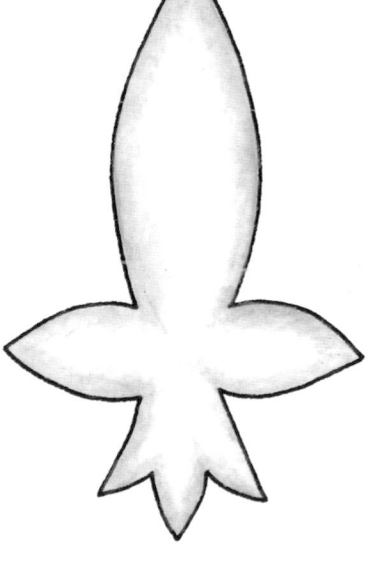

4 Cut a 10 x 11 " piece of sturdy fabric for the lining. Fold it in half and sew the short sides to form a pocket. Insert the pocket into the pencil case. Fold the top edge of the lining in under the zip and slipstitch it in place.

PROJECT 20

Advent Tree

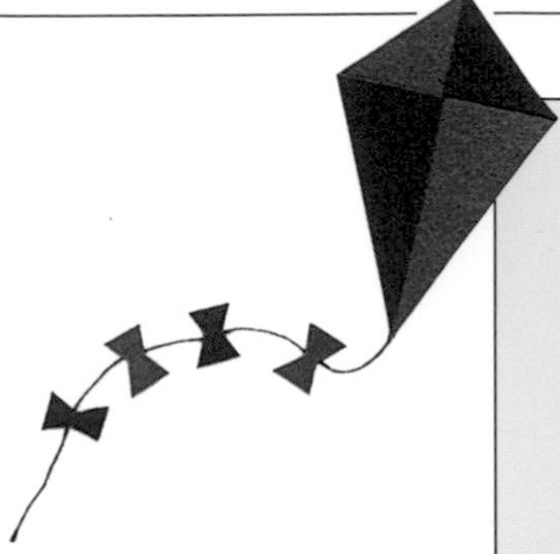

Give children a traditional treat as they count down the twenty-four days to Christmas. This advent tree bears an extra gift, for the big day itself.

YOU WILL NEED

colored fabrics
backing fabric
wadding
ribbons
ornaments
dowel
acrylic paint
a brush
a sewing machine
sewing equipment.

1 ◄ Cut twenty-five 2¾ " squares of fabric with pinking shears. For each of these pockets, cut two pieces of narrow ribbon, arrange them to form a cross and tack them at each end. Sew a ¼ " hem along the top edge of each pocket and iron a matching fold along the remaining edges.

2 ◄ Enlarge the tree pattern on page 158 (see page 14) so that it is 29½ " high. Cut a tree each from green fabric and from backing fabric. Lay the two pieces together, right sides facing, and sew a ½ " seam, leaving a gap. Turn the tree section right side out. Cut wadding slightly smaller than the tree shape, insert it, and handsew the gap closed.

3 ◄ Arrange the pockets on the tree and pin them in place. Sew each pocket along the sides and base. Cut a 24 x 36 " piece of cream backing fabric and sew a ½ " hem on all edges. Sew a 1 " casing at the top and base. Pin the tree onto the backing and sew ½ " in from the edge of the tree.

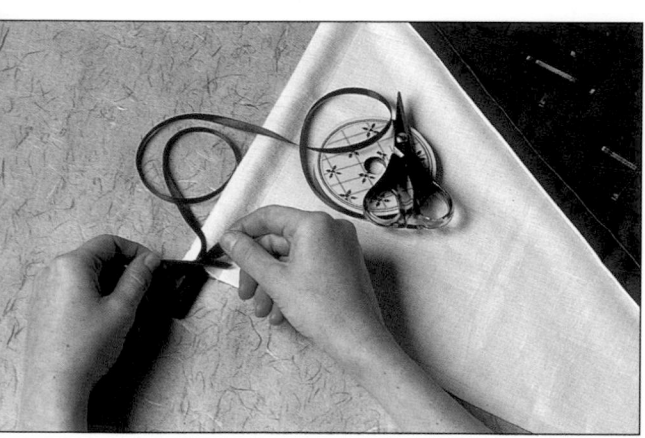

4 ◄ Cut two 28 " lengths of ½ " dowel and apply a coat of red acrylic paint. When the paint is dry, thread a dowel through each of the casings. Attach a long ribbon at the top for hanging and tie bows at the base to secure the dowel.

PROJECT 21

Cot Cover

The moon and stars are fitting companions for a sleeping child, and they shine very brightly on this charming cot quilt.

YOU WILL NEED
colored fabrics
wadding
paper
a pencil
embroidery threads
sewing equipment
a sewing machine

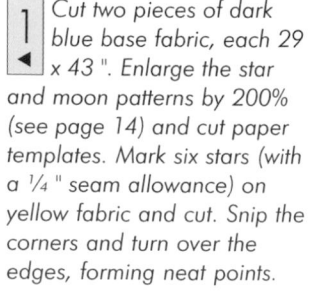

1 ▶ Cut two pieces of dark blue base fabric, each 29 x 43 ". Enlarge the star and moon patterns by 200% (see page 14) and cut paper templates. Mark six stars (with a ¼ " seam allowance) on yellow fabric and cut. Snip the corners and turn over the edges, forming neat points.

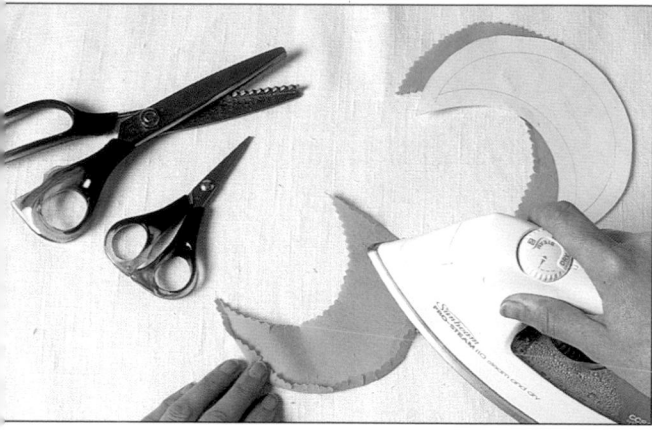

2 ▲ Mark and cut three yellow moons with a seam allowance. Snip at regular intervals around the curve, turn over the seam allowance and press. From pale blue fabric, cut two strips measuring 3 x 37 " and two strips measuring 3 x 25 ". Turn over a ½ " seam allowance and press.

3 ▶ Arrange the appliqué pieces on a base section and tack them in position. Slipstitch around all the appliqué pieces. Lay the two base pieces together, right sides facing, and sew a ½ " seam around three edges. Turn the quilt right side out. Cut wadding to fit and insert it in the quilt.

Suggestion: If the blue background shows throught the yellow fabric, use interfacing in the stars and moons. This will also make the appliqué work easier.

4 ▶ Pin the layers at the corners, securing the wadding in place. At the corners of the pale blue frame and in the center of each motif, make a tiny stitch with embroidery thread, starting and ending at the back. Tie securely and trim to leave a tuft. Slipstitch the fourth side of the quilt closed.

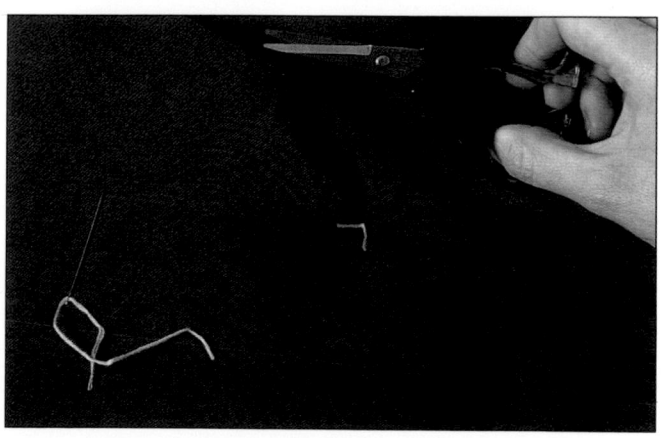

Quilting

There is a degree of confusion surrounding quilting, in relation to the crafts of patchwork and appliqué. The three techniques are often combined in quilt making, but the actual quilting is simply the process of sandwiching three layers—the top, the filler, and the backing—and securing them together.

Having said that, it doesn't mean that quilting is a purely functional technique: the quilting stitches can often be a decorative feature of a project. Quilting is usually worked with a series of small, even running stitches and these can be sewn in regular patterns, such as diamonds or overlapping circles, or in designs which either enhance a decorated top fabric or are the sole decoration. Projects 22 and 23 on the following pages are examples of the latter. The simplest form of quilting, and one which has no embellishing function but is designed instead to be invisible, is "tufting" or tied quilting. This is the quilting method used in the cot cover featured in Project 21.

For all other types, mark quilting lines with a fine line, drawn in either tailor's chalk or dissolvable pen. Polyester wadding or batting is commonly used as interlining or filler in quilting. It is sold in large rolls of varying thicknesses, the thickest being suitable for tufting only. Wadding is also made from natural fibers, such as cotton and silk, but these are more expensive and can be more difficult to quilt.

Quilting work can be stitched by hand or by machine; the first is a therapeutic craft, the second is a practical shortcut. Hand quilting can be done on your lap or with the work fixed in a frame. Keep one hand under the work and the other on top and guide the needle back and forth.

These pieces show some of the ways in which quilting can be applied. The appliqué heart has been stitched on during the quilting process. Quilting stitches can be worked in regular patterns to create a background or as feature motifs.

Quilting is ideal for making warm garments such as jackets. Here, satin patchwork has been quilted by the tufting method.

PROJECT 22

Play Pillow

YOU WILL NEED
pale fabric
backing fabric
wadding
embroidery thread
a marker
fiber filler
sewing equipment
a sewing machine

*Here is a charming companion for those afternoon naps.
By adding a zip and lining, you could turn this project
into a pajamas case.*

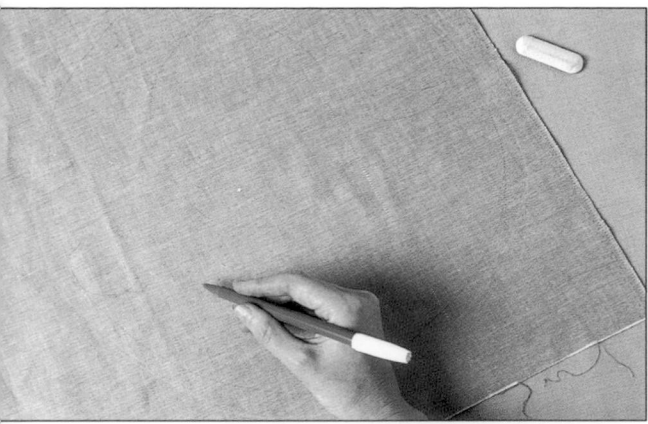

1 ◄ Enlarge the pattern to the desired size (see page 14) and transfer it onto the colored fabric with a dissolving marker or tailor's chalk. Flip the design and mark up another section for the reverse side of the pillow. Cut out the pieces, with a 1" allowance around the design.

2 ▲ Cut wadding and backing fabric to the same size and pin these together with a marked colored piece on top. Thread a needle with embroidery thread and, starting with the ear, stitch along the design lines with long, even stitches. Quilt both marked pieces in this way and then staystitch the edges.

3 ◄ Cut a colored band 4" wide and 2" longer than the perimeter of your quilted sections. Staystitch the edges. Lay the band on a quilted section, right sides facing, and sew a ½" seam. Repeat this with the other quilted section, ensuring that the designs are aligned on the front and back.

4 ► Turn the pillow through the gap in the side band. Fill it with polyester fiber filler. Turn the edges of the side band in and slipstitch the opening closed. Remove any traces of marker with a brush or damp sponge.

PROJECT 23

Bottle Cover

YOU WILL NEED
pale fabric
lining fabric
wadding
paper
a pencil
a marker
a hot water bottle
sewing equipment

A hot water bottle is a wonderful thing on cold nights and, while they are not things of great beauty, yours can be made a little more attractive with a quilted cover.

1 Lay a hot water bottle on paper and draw around it with a generous allowance. Cut and use this paper template to cut two pieces from pale fabric and two from lining fabric. Transfer the quilting pattern onto the pale sections, by tracing or by sketching it. Note that only half the pattern is given here.

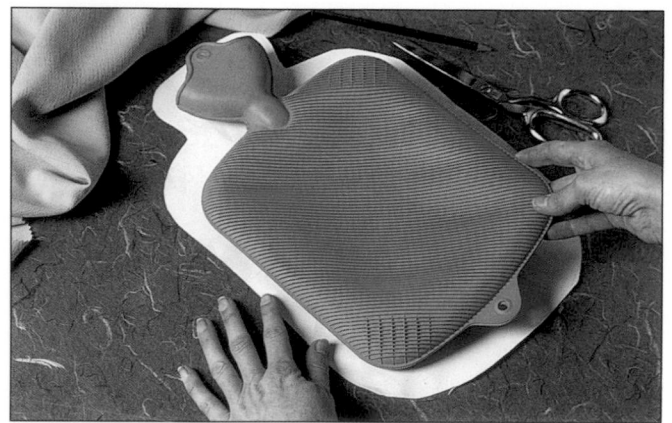

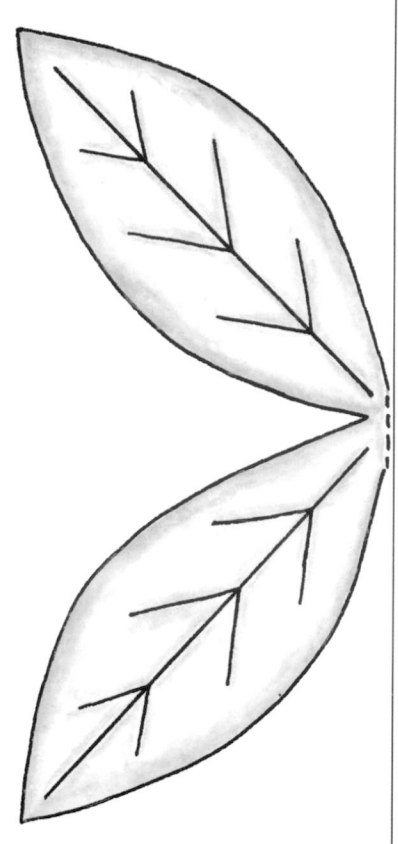

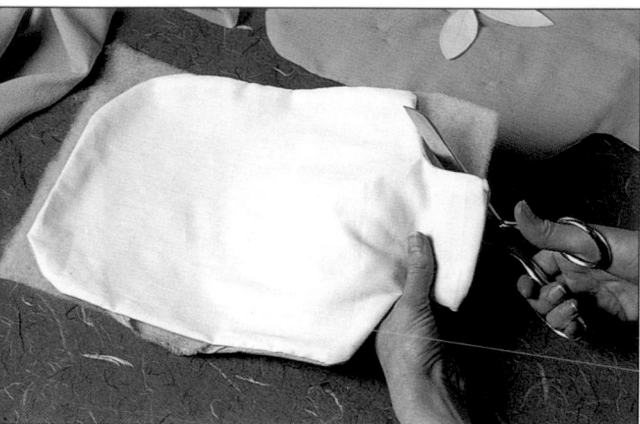

2 Lay a top section and a lining section right sides together and sew a ½ " seam around the edge, leaving the base unsewn. Snip darts at the curves of the corners and at the neck. Turn the side section right side out and cut a piece of wadding to fit inside. Insert it, then slipstitch the gap closed.

3 Pin the three layers together around the quilting pattern. Starting at the center of the design for each leaf, handsew a series of lines with small, even running stitches. At the end of each line make a neat double stitch to secure the stitching, and jump to a nearby section at the back so that it cannot be seen from the front.

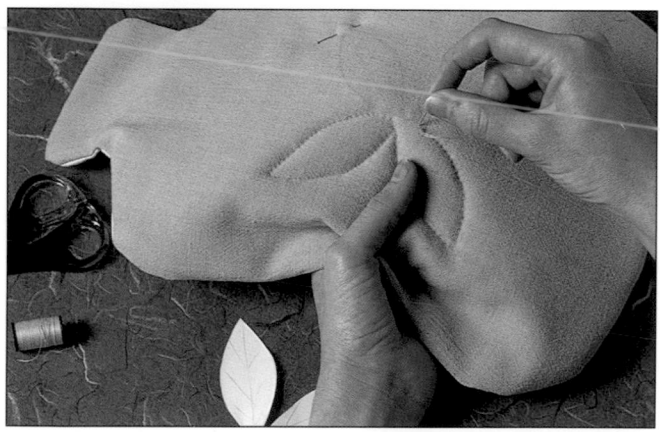

4 Complete each of the two sides separately. Remove any visible quilting marks with a damp sponge or a brush. Pin the two sides together with a bottle in between and handsew around the sides and shoulders. Leave a gap at the base for removing the bottle if you want to wash the cover.

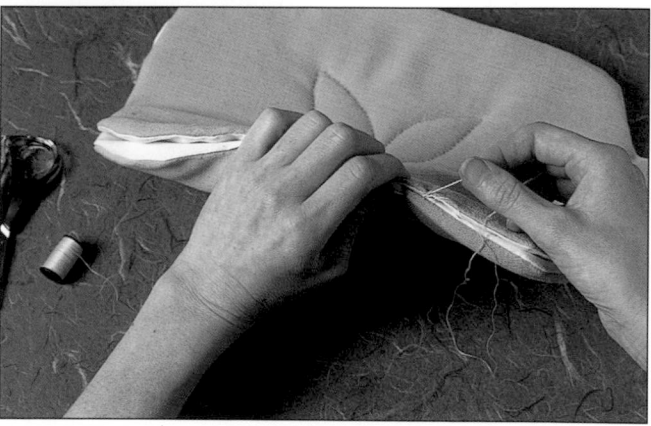

PROJECT 24

Jewelry Roll

Your most precious jewelry will be both well protected and beautifully showcased in this stunning quilted roll.

YOU WILL NEED

silk or satin fabric
backing fabric
wadding
press stud
decorative cord
masking tape
a sewing machine
sewing equipment

1 ▶ Cut a piece of top fabric and two pieces of backing fabric, each 8 x 19½ ". Cut wadding 7 x 18½ ". Tack these layers together: top fabric, backing, wadding, backing. Mark out diagonal quilting lines with masking tape. Machine along the lines. Mark and machine lines along the opposite diagonal.

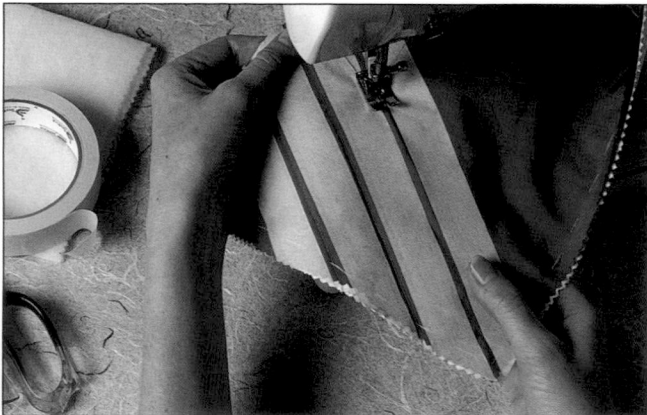

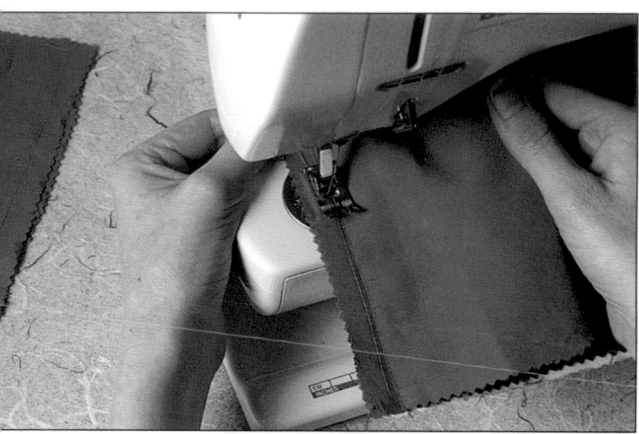

2 Cut two pockets, each 8 x 8 ". Fold pockets in half, wrong sides together, and tack the ragged edges in place on the right side of the top fabric: one on end and the other in the middle.

Lay the ring strap across the roll so that the open end lies at the raw edge. Tack it in place at the raw edge and attach a press stud fastener at the other end.

3 ▲ Cut 35 " of fine cord and knot both ends. Fold the cord in half and secure it at one short end of the roll. Cut a 1½ x 7½ " piece of top fabric for the ring strap. Fold it in half lengthwise and sew a ¼ " seam along one short end and the long side. Turn the fabric tube right side out and poke a long strip of wadding into it with a pencil.

5 ◄ Fold the roll in half, right sides together, and sew along the sides, leaving an opening at the top for turning. Turn the roll right side out and slipstitch the opening closed.

Fabric Sculpture

We tend to think of fabric as a two-dimensional material, given shape only when used to cover another object. Quilting is one way we can create depth using fabric, but there are others. Pleating, gathering, folding, smocking: all create shadows and a three-dimensional effect and have been used for centuries to enhance clothing.

Pleats are even folds, usually with sharp edges, which can be set in a variety of ways. They reduce the width of the fabric, while giving it a very tactile dimension. Smocking, a combination of pleating and embroidery, has evolved from a practical means of gathering to a decorative technique. Another way to add interest is by attaching tassels. While they are not strictly made by sculpting fabric, the use of bound threads makes them a close relation. Tasselmaking has become immensely popular over the last few years and Project 26 offers a simple introduction.

Another technique which has gained a following is the use of a stiffening medium to help fabric hold a shape. Soft fabrics, such as muslin, take this treatment well and can be transformed into dramatic drapes, bows and lampshades quite inexpensively. If the fabric is new, wash it first to remove any dressing. Equal parts of white glue and water are recommended for most projects: for a stiffer finish use less water or none at all. See the next page for more information.

The natural extension to this idea is fabric mâché, in which small scraps of fabric are pasted together to form all sorts of unlikely shapes. This virtually unexplored territory offers great potential to the adventurous!

Fabric can be manipulated in many ways to give it an extra dimension or added texture.

Fabric stiffener
Bottles of fabric stiffener are available commercially but it is much cheaper to make your own by mixing equal parts of water and white glue. Work with a soft fabric and dampen it first by spraying, then brush on enough stiffener to saturate the fabric. Arrange it in the desired shape and leave it to dry overnight.

To make silk freesias, first paint the fabric with silk paint and allow it to dry. Cut the silk into the required shape, here a rectangle with petal sections at the top. Heat a rounded object and press it into each petal to shape it. Roll the base of the rectangle loosely and bind it with a fine wire. Cover the wire with stem tape. Bind a series of such flowers in decreasing sizes to make a spray.

PROJECT 25

Potpourri Sack

YOU WILL NEED

fabric
cord
fabric stiffener
a wide brush
a bottle
plastic wrap
an elastic band
sewing equipment

A pretty sack shaped with fabric stiffener makes a wonderful container for potpourri. You could substitute hessian for a natural look, or a rich tapestry for extra class.

1 ► Cut two pieces of fabric, each 8 x 14 ". Place right sides together and sew along three edges. Trim corners and iron seams open. From the top edge, measure and fold 5 " of fabric back to form a false lining inside the bag.

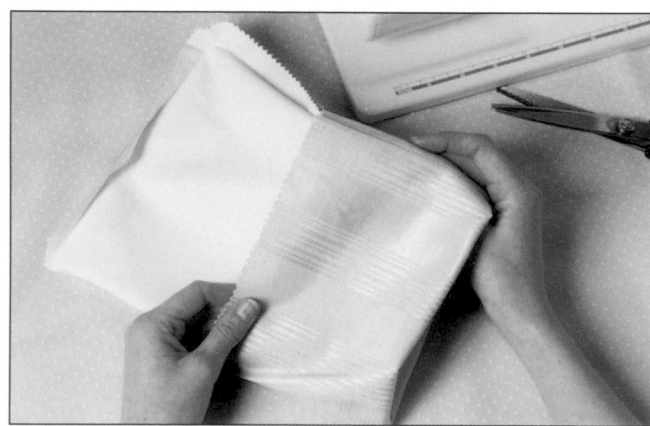

2 ► Cover your work space with a sheet of plastic. If a commercial fabric stiffener is not available, thin white glue with water. Apply a generous coat of stiffener to the inside of the bag with a wide brush. Turn the bag right side out and apply another coat of stiffener.

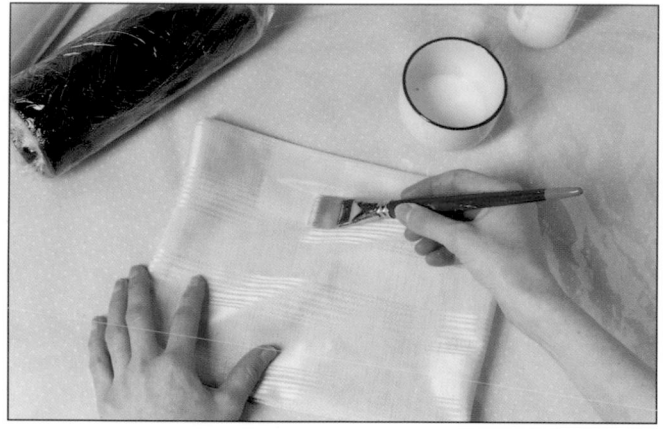

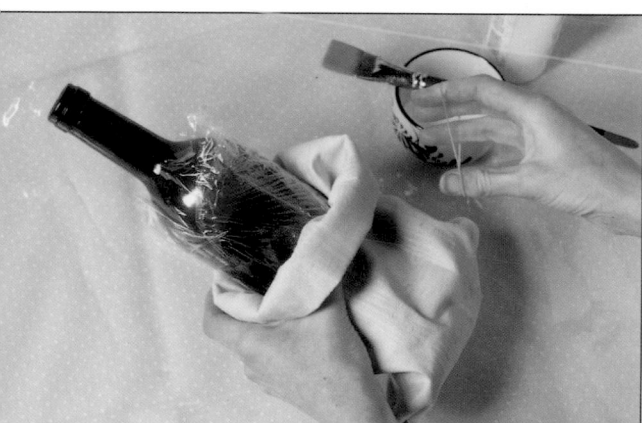

3 ◄ Cover a bottle with plastic wrap to prevent the bag sticking to it. Slip the damp bag over the base of the bottle and stretch a large elastic band around the neck. Arrange the bag loosely and allow it to dry in that position.

4 ◄ When the bag is completely dry, remove the elastic band and slip the bag off the bottle. Tie a length of silk cord or ribbon loosely around the neck of the bag and fill it with potpourri.

PROJECT 26

Gift Stocking

YOU WILL NEED
red velvet
paper
cardboard
a pencil
a ruler
gold cord
embroidery thread
sewing equipment

Tassels give an otherwise plain item an extra dimension in this delightful Christmas stocking. They are quick to make and can be used to decorate countless fabric projects.

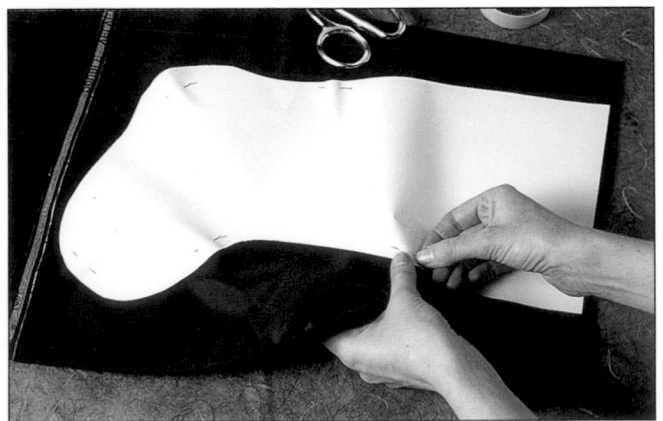

1 ◄ *Enlarge the stocking pattern by approximately 300% and transfer it onto a piece of paper (see page 14). Fold a piece of red velvet in half and use the paper template to cut the shape from the two layers. With right sides facing, sew a ½ " seam around the stocking, leaving the top unsewn. Staystitch the raw edges. Fold the top edge over and make a deep hem.*

2 ◄ *Turn the stocking right side out. Pin a length of gold cord along the seam and form a hanging loop at the top back of the stocking. Neatly handsew the cord onto the velvet with small stitches in a thread which matches the cord.*

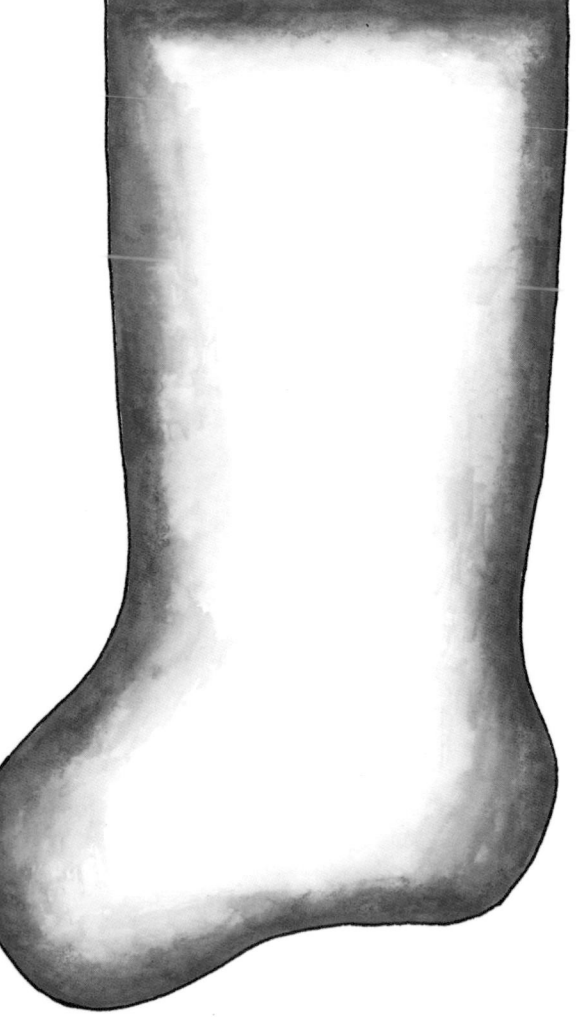

3 ▲ *Cut a cardboard strip 2 " wide and lay a short piece of embroidery thread along it. Wind another length of thread around the card 25 times. Knot the ends of the short piece so that the loops are gathered tightly. Slip them off the card and wind another thread tightly around the neck of the tassel. Trim the loops.*

Attach each tassel to the stocking with the two loose ties and knot them together on the inside of the stocking.

PROJECT 27

Pen Holder

YOU WILL NEED
heavy muslin
colored fabrics
a jar
petroleum jelly
white glue
a wide brush
scissors

Fabrics which are absorbent will behave much like paper when glue is applied, opening up the many possibilities offered by the craft of papier-mâché.

1 ▶ Lay newspaper or plastic sheeting over the work area. Coat the base and sides of a jar with petroleum jelly. Cut a large number of squares, roughly 1 " square in size, from strong muslin or linen.

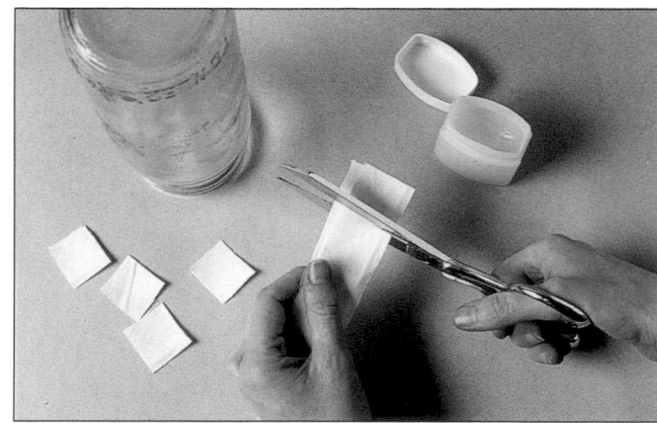

2 ▶ Make a paste by adding 1 part water to 2 parts white glue. Dip fabric squares in the paste and remove excess paste with your fingers. Lay squares on the base of the jar, overlapping them and smoothing each one down with your fingertips. Continue adding overlapping pieces, working your way down the sides of the jar until it is the desired height.

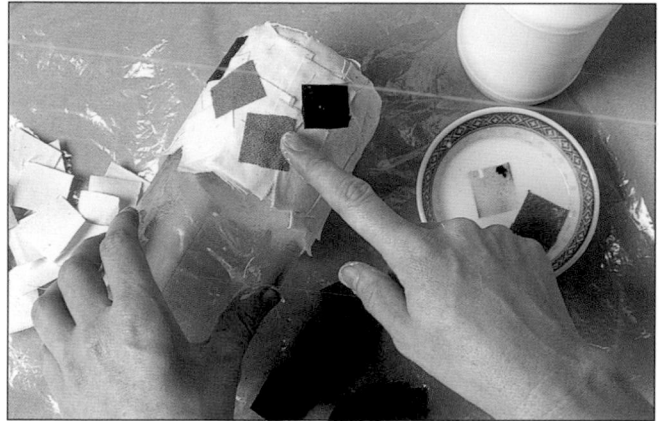

3 ◀ Repeat the previous step, adding a second layer of squares, and a third and fourth layer if the fabric is thin. Cut squares of fabrics in contrasting colors, soak them in the paste and apply them on the sides as decoration. Leave the project until the outside is dry, then lift it carefully off the jar.

4 ▶ Cut a piece of lining fabric which will fit loosely inside the pot. Apply a coat of paste to both sides of this piece with a wide brush. Arrange the coated lining in the pot so that it can accommodate pencils and leave the project to dry completely.

Cartonnage

The craft of making fabric-covered boxes was especially popular in 19th century France and it is currently enjoying something of a resurgence. Boxes (and their contents) appeal to our curiosity and there are few better ways of storing odds and ends than in a set of attractive boxes. The same techniques used to cover boxes can be applied to frames, desk sets, portfolios, and countless other items, letting you make full use of the wonderful array of printed fabrics available.

As in any craft, you will find that fabrics with natural fibers are easier to manipulate and cotton is the easiest. Choose prints to suit the project and its probable setting. Avoid checks or stripes if they will need to be carefully aligned.

You can choose to make your own boxes, using pieces of stiff cardboard and tape, or you may prefer to recycle old containers. When using old boxes, you may need to cover them first with pieces of white paper to conceal any bright colors or printed writing. Making boxes from scratch means that you can create all sorts of shapes, including hexagonals, ovals, and heart-shapes. Simply cut a base to the desired shape, cut the sides and join the sections together with tape.

A layer of thin wadding between the cardboard and the fabric softens the lines of the object and makes it nicer to handle. Glue sticks and spray adhesives are handy for fixing fabric onto cardboard. White glue can seep through a thin fabric and spoil it, but it can be useful for sticking down heavier fabrics, or for attaching braids.

Once you have covered a few projects, you can try combining cartonnage with other techniques from this book. Marbled fabrics, patchwork, and appliqué can all be used for covering; beading or embroidery can be added to embellish plain fabrics.

Tree decorations
These little gifts are made from covered squares of cardboard glued together and tied round with ribbon.

Cardboard is not the only material you can cover with fabric. Some craft stores sell shapes made of polystyrene or plastic which can be used as a base for decorations.

Chateleines
These strings of sewing accessories were popular from the 17th to the 19th century. Designed to hang from the belt of a needle-woman, they became something of a fashion item. This one, featuring a scissors case, pinwheel, needlebook and thimble holder, is made from cardboard shapes covered with embroidered pieces of fabric.

PROJECT 28

Notebook

YOU WILL NEED
a bound notebook
fabric
double-sided tape
thin wadding
scissors

*A plain notebook or diary can be turned into a thing of beauty
with a fabric covering. Choose a material which does not
easily fray, or apply a fray-check liquid around the edges.*

1 Cut a piece of wadding that will wrap around your notebook or diary. Lay strips of double-sided tape around the edges of the cover and tape the wadding down smoothly, then trim the edges if necessary.

2 Cut a piece of fabric sufficiently larger than the book to allow a 1 " turnover at all edges. Lay strips of double-sided tape around the edges of the book's inside cover.

3 Wrap the fabric around the book and secure it evenly at the sides. At the top, make two angled snips at the book's spine and fold the V shape back between the fabric and the book. Repeat this at the base of the book.

4 Cut a dart at one of the corners and fold a tuck in the fabric, then secure this with double-sided tape. Repeat this for each corner, making sure that the covering lies smooth over the book.

PROJECT 29

Picture Frame

This stylish double frame can be sized to suit your own cherished photographs. A small floral print is ideal for such a project.

YOU WILL NEED
stiff cardboard
fabric
interfacing
spray adhesive
white glue
a ruler
a pencil
a knife & mat
sewing equipment

1 The picture area of your photographs is A (height) x B (width). Cut four pieces of cardboard, each A+2½ " x B+2½ ". In two of these, cut a window the same size as the picture area. Cut three pieces of fabric, each A+4 " x 2B+4 ".

2 Cut one of the fabric pieces in half and lay it right side down. Lay a frame on top and mark the corners of the window with a pen. Make a cut in the center of the fabric and snip towards the corner marks. Spray the frame with adhesive and lay it in position on the fabric. Turn the flaps over the edges, trim if necessary, and glue down. Glue the other frame onto the other half of the fabric.

3 Lay another fabric piece face down. Spray the other two cardboard pieces lightly and place them on the fabric, ¾ " apart. Snip a triangle from each of the fabric corners, turn the flaps and glue them down. At each corner on this and on the frames, dab some glue to prevent fraying.

4 Stiffen the middle of the third piece of fabric with a strip of interfacing. Fold over the edges all around so that it is slightly smaller than the backing section. Position the lining section face up on the backing section and slipstitch around the edges.

5 Place a window section on top of the backing to one side, and slipstitch around the three outside edges to secure it in place. Repeat with the other window, positioning it on the other extreme of the backing. Carefully insert photographs.

PROJECT 30

Treasure Chest

Covering a box requires a plenty of fabric and a degree of patience but the results are worthwhile, especially if you're making a treasure chest.

YOU WILL NEED
a shoebox
hessian
wadding
white glue
a toggle
shells
raffia
a drill
sewing equipment

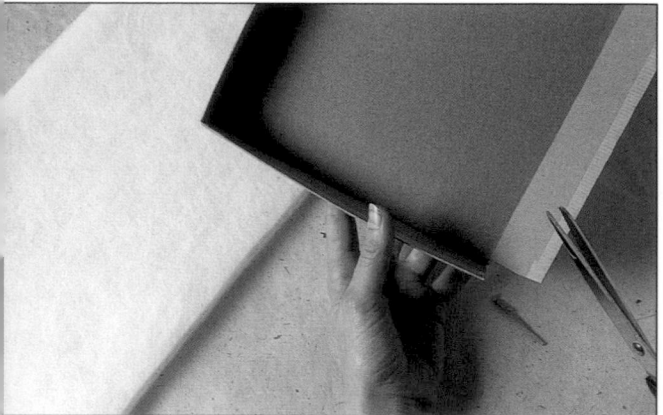

1 You will need a strong cardboard box with a loose-fitting lid and a large piece of hessian. Take the lid and snip two of the corners as shown to form the back hinge. Cut a piece of wadding to fit the top of the lid and fix it on with a thin layer of white glue.

3 Cover the lid with a separate piece of fabric, leaving a flap along one edge. Trim the excess fabric at the back of the box. Glue the snipped "hinge" of the lid onto the inside back of the box. Glue the fabric flap at the back of the lid over the fabric on the box, ensuring that the lid opens easily.

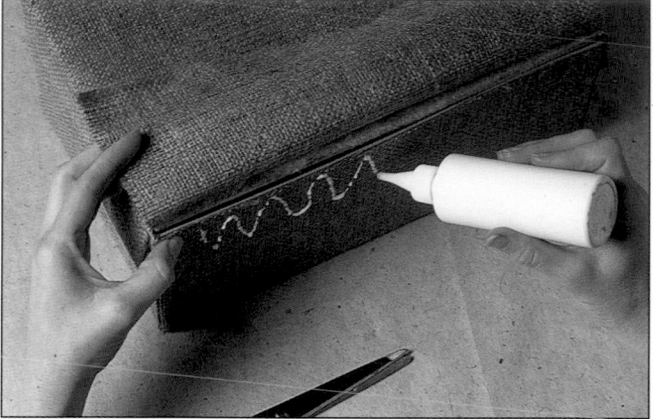

2 Apply glue to the box base and place it on the fabric. At the narrow ends, cut the fabric to fit the base, allowing for flaps at either side. Apply glue onto the ends and wrap the fabric over them, gluing the flaps down on the front and back. Cut and glue the front and back sections. Fold the excess fabric over the rim at the sides and front and glue down.

4 Use a heavy-duty needle and strong raffia to attach a wooden toggle or other fastener to the center front of the box, and knot the raffia on the inside of the box. Fasten a short piece of raffia to the center rim of the lid so it can be wound around the toggle. Line the inside of the box with fabric or brown paper.

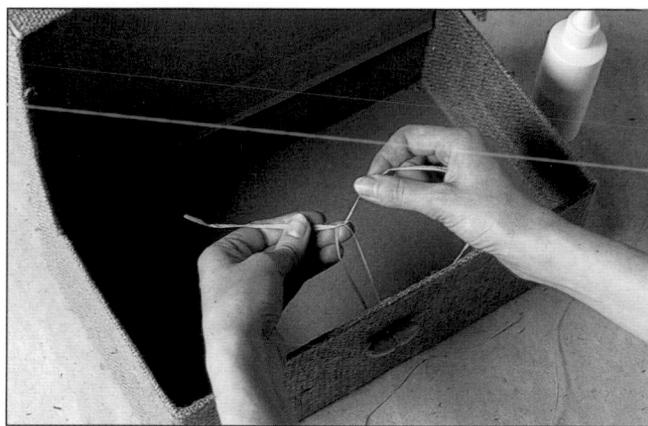

5 Drill small holes in an array of shells, or select plastic jewels with holes in them. Attach these as decorations to the top of the lid, using fine pieces of raffia or strong gold thread.

Painting

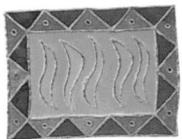

Decorating fabric with paint doesn't require any great artistic ability and is a lot of fun. You can paint anything from a simple repeat motif on a t-shirt to a blaze of color on a silk scarf—all you need are the appropriate paints and a little bit of planning.

A touch of paint is a good way to revitalise old clothing or to turn plain, inexpensive fabric into striking table linen, curtains, or lampshades. The best fabrics to paint are those with natural fibers, as synthetic fabrics are unpredictable in the way they receive paint. Fine silk is particularly delightful to paint on and can be bought in small squares for that purpose.

Newly bought fabric should be washed before paint is applied, to remove any dressing and so encourage it to absorb the paint. A good ironing for both new and old fabrics removes any wrinkles and creases which might spoil your painting.

There is now a wide array of paints designed specifically for applying to fabrics. These include ones with pearl or metallic finishes and some which puff up when heat is applied. Most are water-based and non-toxic, an important consideration if children are likely to be using them. As most fabric paints are sold in small containers, it can become an expensive affair, so it is worth investing in a bottle of textile medium formulated to combine with acrylic paints and make them suitable for application on fabrics.

Some types of fabric paint have to be fixed so that they are color-fast and the item can be washed repeatedly. This is often done by ironing the wrong side of the painted fabric, but follow the instructions provided by the manufacturer.

Textile medium can be added to most acrylic paints so that they can be used on fabrics.

Silk painting
Intensely colored water-based paints are available for painting on silk. These are free-flowing and so need to be contained by gutta, an outliner paste which blocks the mesh of the fabric. Clear gutta is washed out afterwards, but metallic gutta, used in this example, becomes a feature of the design.

Colorful clothing
The fine nozzles on most bottles of ready-mixed fabric paints are ideal for drawing patterns and pictures on small items of clothing, such as sox, caps, shoes and t-shirts.

Beads
Paint a piece of silk or other fine fabric. Cut a long strip, fold it length-wise and seam along one edge. Turn the tube and thread one end through a jump ring, then push a lightweight bead into the tube. Add another jump ring and bead, and so on.

97

Spatter Pillows

YOU WILL NEED
*white pillowcases
stiff cardboard
masking tape
newspaper
fabric paints
a nail brush
a wide paint brush*

*A set of pillowcases spattered with bright fabric paints is
an attractive decorating feature during the day. At night,
simply turn the pillows over for sleeping.*

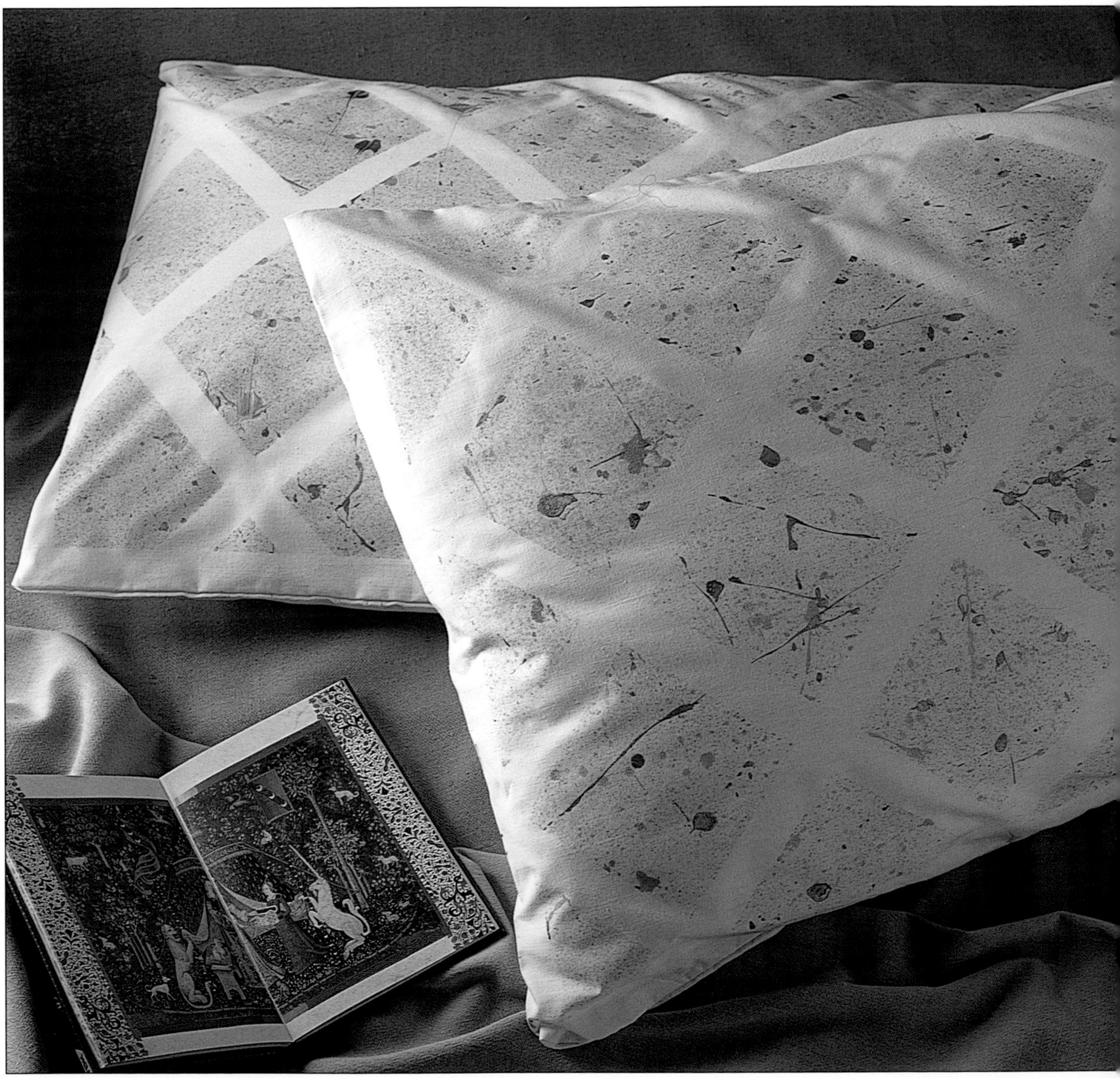

1 ▶ If the pillowcases are new, wash them thoroughly to remove any size and then iron them. Cut a piece of cardboard slightly smaller than your pillow and insert it into a pillowcase. Place a small piece of cardboard under the flap of the pillowcase: this will prevent the layers from sticking together.

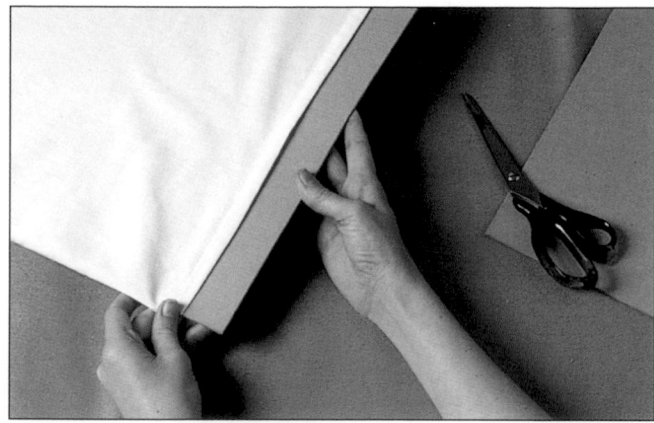

2 ▶ Lay a strip of masking tape around the edges of the case. Cut a strip of paper 4" wide and use this as a template to lay diagonal strips of masking tape at regular intervals. Lay another set of diagonal strips so that a diamond pattern is created.

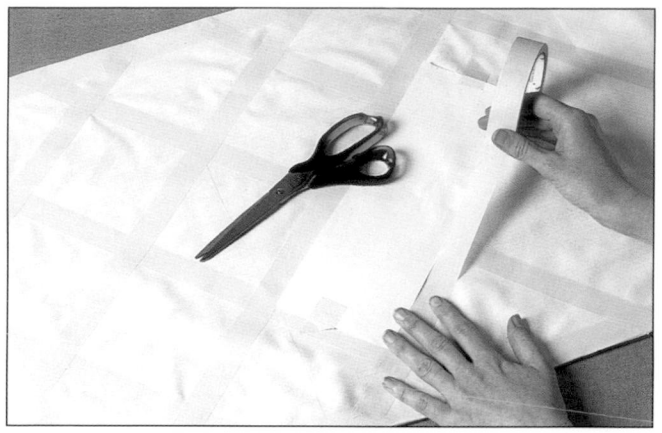

3 ▶ Place the pillowcase on sheets of newspaper. Dip a nailbrush in a generous amount of fabric paint and run your finger over the bristles so that paint is sprayed onto the fabric: you may prefer to use a knife for this task. Continue until you are satisfied with the coverage of paint, reloading the nailbrush with paint as necessary.

4 ◀ Dip a large paintbrush in another color of fabric paint and flick your wrist so that paint spatters onto the fabric. If this creates large blobs, try thinning the paint slightly with water. When you are happy with the design, leave the pillowcase to dry. Remove the masking tape and set the paint as per the manufacturer's instructions.

PROJECT 32

Greeting Cards

Metallic "gutta" or outliner adds to the richness of the silk paints in these jewel-like cards. You can experiment with color combinations using the one design.

YOU WILL NEED
fine silk
metallic gutta
silk paints
polystyrene or board
pins
a marker & a brush
a nib & bottle
scissors
white cardboard
spray adhesive

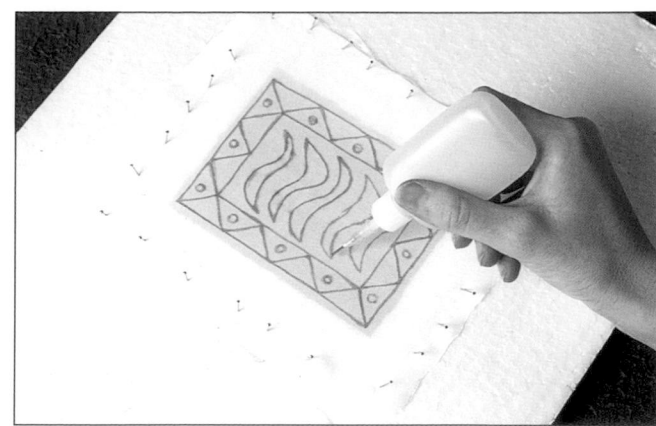

1 Prewash the silk and press it. Lay a piece over the pattern and trace over the lines with a pencil or a dissolving marker. (You may need to trace it onto paper first and then trace it over a window.)

2 In a sheet of polystyrene or cardboard packaging, cut a hole slightly larger than the pattern. Pin the silk so that the design sits over the hole and the silk is taut. Apply metallic gutta along the lines of the design, using a plastic bottle and a large nib. Make sure that all the intersecting lines connect, or paint will escape through the gaps. Allow the gutta to dry.

3 Test your paints on a scrap of silk: thin paints with a little water for a less intense color. Dip the brush in paint and then lightly touch the silk. Complete the sections in one color then rinse your brush and paint the next color.

4 When the paint is dry, iron the silk between two sheets of paper to fix the paint. Trim around the edge of the design with scissors. Spray the back lightly with adhesive and glue it on a folded piece of thin white cardboard.

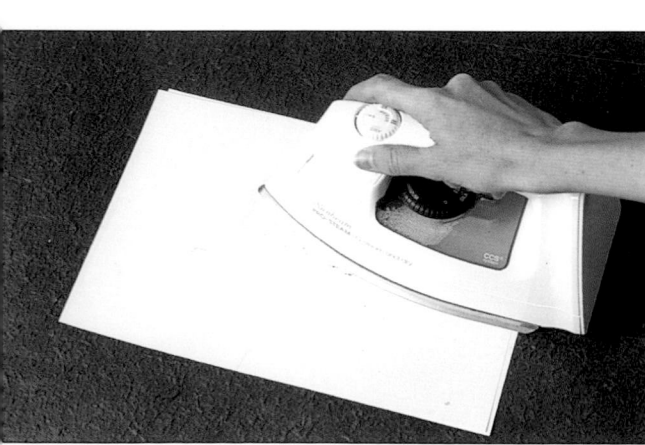

PROJECT 33

Play Mat

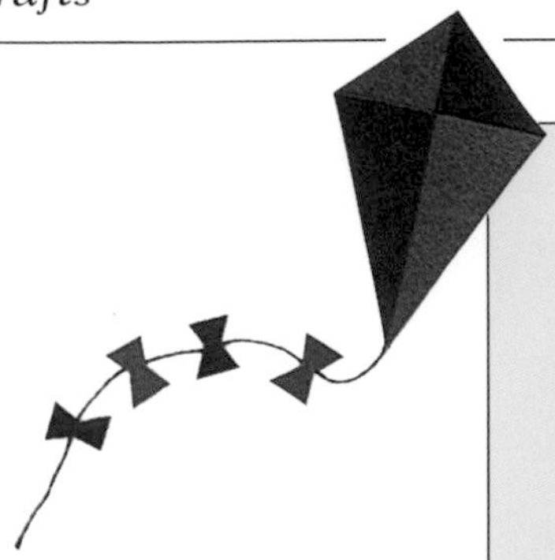

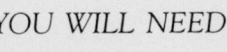

Children will be thrilled when you make this mat and a whole town is laid out at their feet. Better still, engage their help to make it.

YOU WILL NEED
heavy muslin or
    canvas
fabric paints
acrylic varnish
masking tape
a ruler
a marker
several paint brushes
sewing equipment

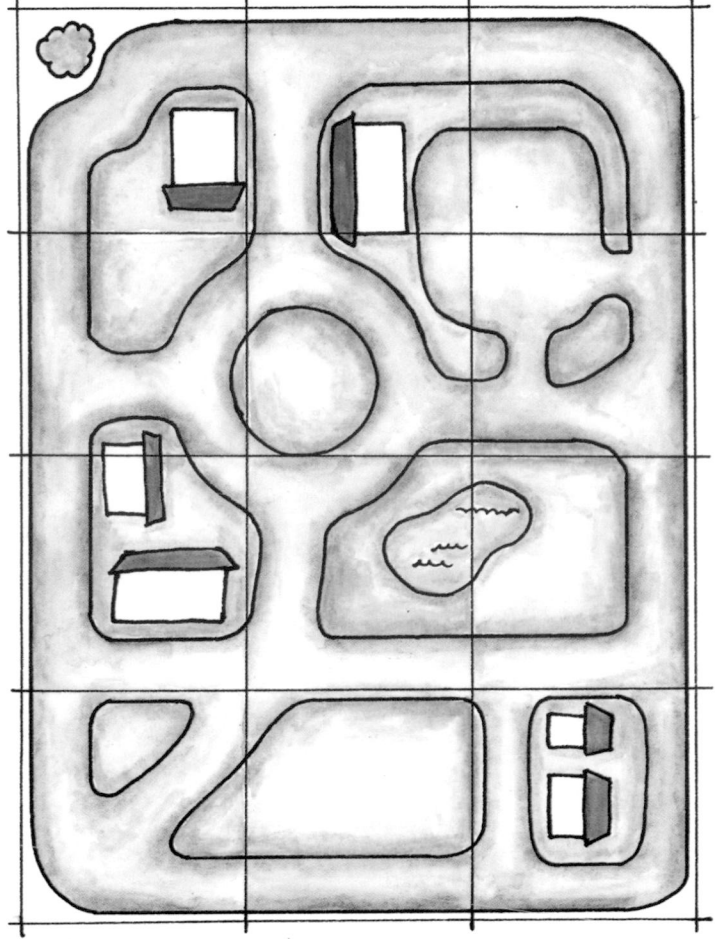

1 ▲ *Cut a piece of canvas or heavy muslin measuring 42 x 29 ". Fold and iron a 1 " hem all around. Fold the fabric in half with hems inside to give a rectangle measuring 20 x 27 ". Mark out a 6¾ " grid on one face, using a ruler and masking tape. Transfer the design, square by square.*

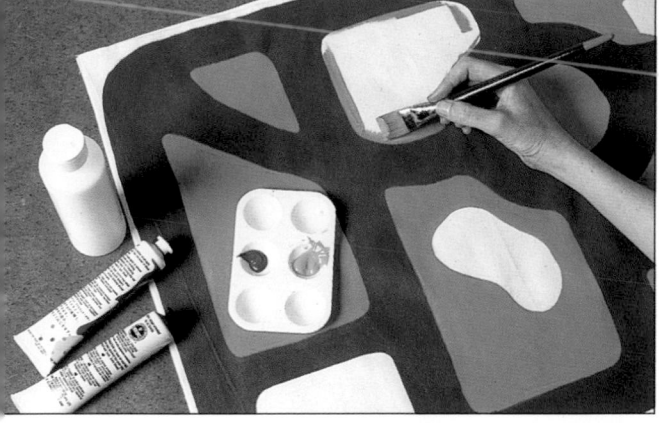

2 ◄ *Place a sheet of plastic between the fabric layers. Use a wide brush to paint gray roads, green areas, and a blue pond. Paint the houses white with red roofs. Allow the paint to dry.*

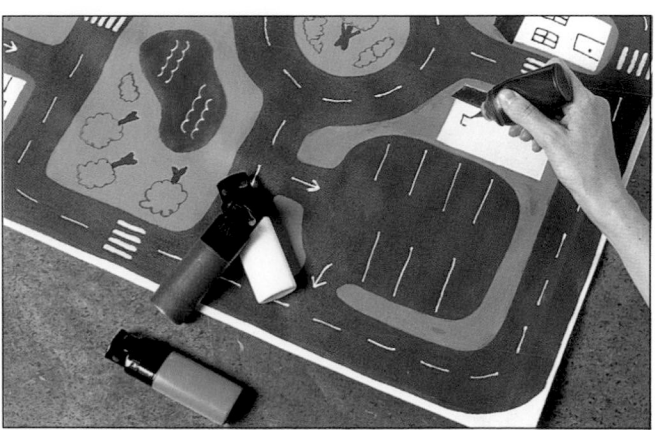

3 ◄ *Add the details with a fine brush or nozzle, painting road markings and pond waves in white, windows and doors in black, and trees in green and brown. When dry, slipstitch the folded edges together with strong thread. Apply several coats of acrylic varnish over the paint.*

Dyeing

Before the mid-19th century, fabrics were dyed with such natural materials as flowers, dried insects, and powdered minerals. The rarest dyes were highly prized—Tyrian purple, made from crushed shellfish, was reserved for the robes of the Roman emperors—and you could often discern someone's status by the color of their clothing. Today, we can still obtain many colors from natural materials. Yellow-gold can be obtained from boiling onion skins, brown from walnut shells, and so on. The colors can be somewhat unpredictable—no two dye batches will be the same—but that is part of the charm of natural dyes.

For the less adventurous, commercial dyes are available in a range of forms, suitable for either hot-water or cold-water dyeing. The latter type is ideal for craft work, especially for batik as the dyeing process will not melt the wax.

Fabrics receive dyes differently, according to the structure of the fibers. In general, fabrics with natural fibers dye better than synthetics. Wool, cotton and silk all have a good affinity for dyes, but linen does not.

A mordant is a chemical which allows the fibers to combine with a dye and fixes the color permanently. Mordanting can be done before, during or after the dyeing process. For natural dyes, alum or cream of tartar are the most commonly used mordants and fabrics should be soaked in a solution of these before dyeing. Commercial dyes specify the mordant that should be added to the dye. Generally this is salt, in combination with a sachet of fixative. In the case of wool, however, this is replaced by vinegar.

There are few rules when dyeing. One is to wear old clothes and rubber gloves, as it can be a very messy procedure. The other is to make notes as you work, so you can replicate the results later!

Tie-dyeing
One way of preventing dye from reaching the fabric is to bind sections tightly with string. Winding string around a strip of fabric will produce stripes, as in Project 35. Binding small clumps of fabric creates undyed circles, like those shown here.

Batik scarf
The process of batik relies on the ability of wax to resist the dye. The wax is applied with instruments called caps, the fabric is dyed, and then the wax is melted with a hot iron and removed. Great care should be taken when working with hot wax.

Natural impressions
Here, leaves have been dipped in hot wax and laid onto silk which is then colored with silk paint.

PROJECT 34

Bunting

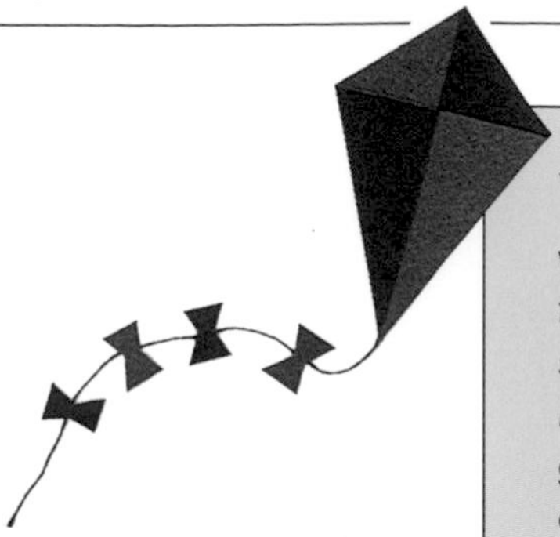

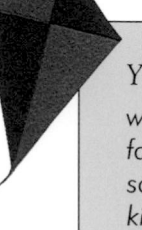

YOU WILL NEED
white cotton fabric
fabric dyes
salt
kitchen utensils
gold thread
cord
a safety pin
a sewing machine
sewing equipment

Here is a simple exercise to get you accustomed to using fabric dyes. The result is a charming string of brightly colored flags, which can be brought out for all special occasions.

1 ▶ Cut white cotton fabric into strips 10 " wide. Mix up cold-water dyes, following the manufacturer's instructions. Immerse fabric in each dye bath, ensuring that it is fully covered and can move freely. Leave the fabric for the recommended time, then rinse the pieces well and hang to dry.

2 ▶ Cut a triangular paper template with two long sides of 10¼ " and a short side of 5¼ ". Alternatively, you can use a 60° triangle. Mark and cut triangles from the colored fabric strips, turning the template around each time so there is no waste.

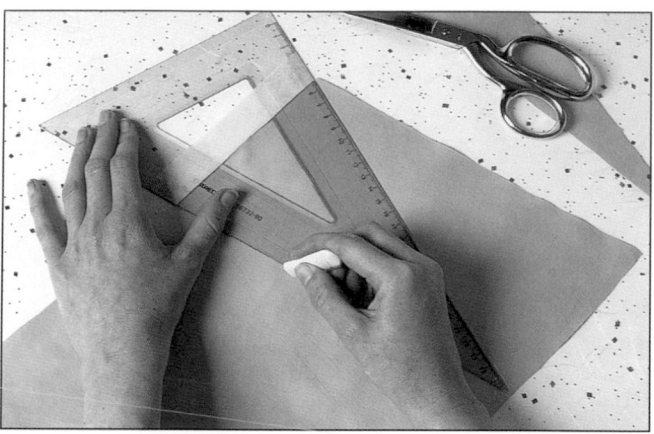

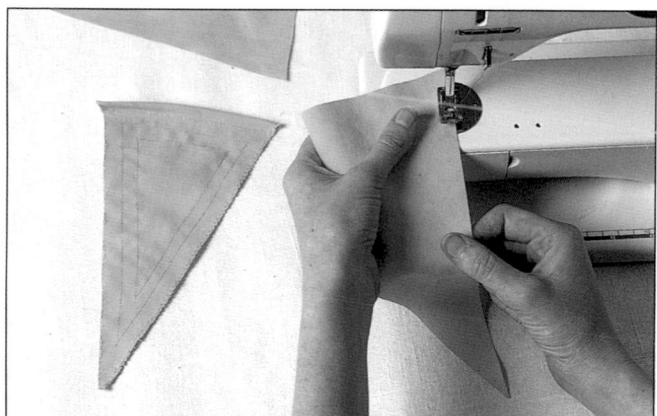

3 ◀ Select a fine gold thread that can be used on a sewing machine and adjust the machine's tension if necessary. Zigzag around the edge of a fabric triangle, then turn the short end over and sew a ¾ " casing with straight stitch. Machine a series of triangles, one within another, for decoration.

4 ▶ Attach a small safety pin to one end of a length of cord and thread it through the casings of the flags. Form a loop at either end of the cord and secure each loop with a few stitches. Stitch the flags in place along the cord if desired.

PROJECT 35

Tie-Dye Tie

A tie is a common gift for a man, but here's one that's rather special. The one shown is made in cotton, but you could also use a heavy silk or a light linen.

YOU WILL NEED
white fabric
lining fabric
string
cold fabric dye
salt
kitchen utensils
a sewing machine
sewing equipment

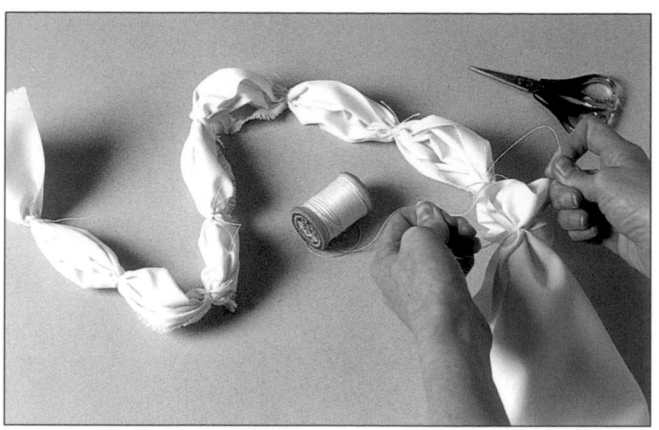

1 Cut a 20 x 30 " piece of white natural fabric such as fine cotton or strong silk. At intervals along its length, bunch the fabric with your hands and bind a piece of string tightly around it several times, securing the ends with a tight knot.

2 Following the dye instructions, mix up a batch in a container so that the fabric will be fully covered and can move freely in the dye bath. Immerse the bound fabric and leave it in the dye for the recommended time. Remove it from the dye, rinse it well and hang it to dry. When the fabric is dry, cut the knots carefully and remove the string.

3 Iron the dyed fabric. Lay an old tie across the fabric diagonally. Use this as a guide to cut a basic shape in three sections, allowing extra fabric at the sides for the back seam. The dyed strip should be roughly two-and-a-half times the width of the tie. Cut lining sections for each end from light fabric.

4 Lay the sections together at right angles and sew to form one long tapering strip. Place lining on one end, right sides together, and sew around the three raw edges. Turn out and repeat for the other end. Fold the tie in half lengthwise with right sides together. Sew a seam from the start of one lined section to the other. Turn the tie through, using a chopstick or a long skewer. Fold the lined sections in to the center, checking that the points are neat, and slipstitch at the center join.

PROJECT 36

Pot Holder

Here is an easy introduction to batik, the use of wax to control the dyeing process. The result, a sunny pot holder, will no doubt prove very handy!

YOU WILL NEED
white cotton fabric
wadding
bias binding
wax
cardboard
cold fabric dyes
salt
kitchen utensils
a sewing machine
sewing equipment

1 Prewash and dry white fabric. Cut four 10 " squares and a matching square of wadding. On two pieces of fabric, mark a circle with a 7 " diameter. Score a piece of strong cardboard twice with a knife, bend it into a triangle and secure this with tape. Cut a piece of strong cardboard tubing. These pieces are known as "caps."

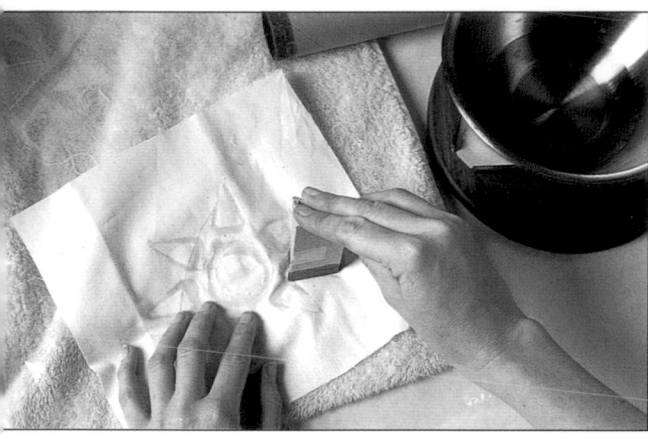

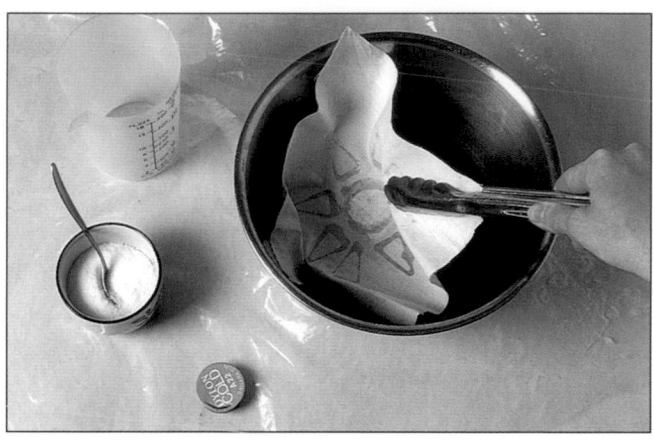

2 Lay a marked square on a folded towel. Melt some wax in a double boiler. Steep the end of the tube in the hot wax and quickly press it on the center of the fabric. The waxed area should darken; if the wax becomes opaque, peel it off and try again when the wax is hotter. With the other cap, mark a ring of triangles around the waxed circle.

3 Wax the other marked square, then turn off the heat. Mix up a small batch of yellow dye. Immerse the waxed fabric squares in the dye bath and leave them for the recommended time, then rinse and hang to dry.

4 Reheat the wax and mark another ring of triangles around the first on each of the squares, staying within the marked circle. Mix up a batch of red dye and dye the fabric squares as before. When they have been rinsed and dried, place each square between two sheets of clean paper and press with a hot iron to remove the wax.

5 Back each batik square with wadding and a lining, and pin to secure. Tack along the circle outline. Trim the layers ¼ " out from the tacking. Form a loop of bias binding and pin this at the edge. Fold bias binding lengthwise and pin it around the edge. Stitch to secure.

Marbling

Marbling is an ancient method of decorating paper and fabric and the skills involved have been highly prized and often closely guarded throughout history. It is easy to see why: there are few forms of decoration more beautiful than the swirls and patterns of a well-marbled piece. Years of practise may be required to achieve such perfection, but meanwhile we can create some delightful effects and have a lot of fun doing so.

The simplest way to marble fabric is by using specially formulated inks which float on water. These are sold in kits of several colors, which can be swirled across a tray of water in pleasing combinations.

The piece of fabric you can marble is limited by the size of your tray. Cat-litter trays or photographic ones are ideal. You will also need a lot of newspaper and some implements for manipulating the paint.

To achieve full control over the paints and so create complex patterns, it is necessary to suspend them on a thick size. Traditionally, this is made from carrageen moss, but the preparation is quite complicated. A good compromise is to work on a thin wallpaper paste or a size of methyl cellulose, which will give some control over the paint's movement.

Either oil paints or fabric paints can be floated on a size but only the latter are suitable on items that must be washed. If using acrylic paints, the fabric must first be washed to remove the dressing and then soaked in an alum solution and allowed to dry, a process called "mordanting" which fixes the color.

While not strictly a marbling technique, the application of coarse salt on silk paints produces another interesting effect. Like marbling, the result is always slightly unpredictable, an element which makes the process all the more exciting!

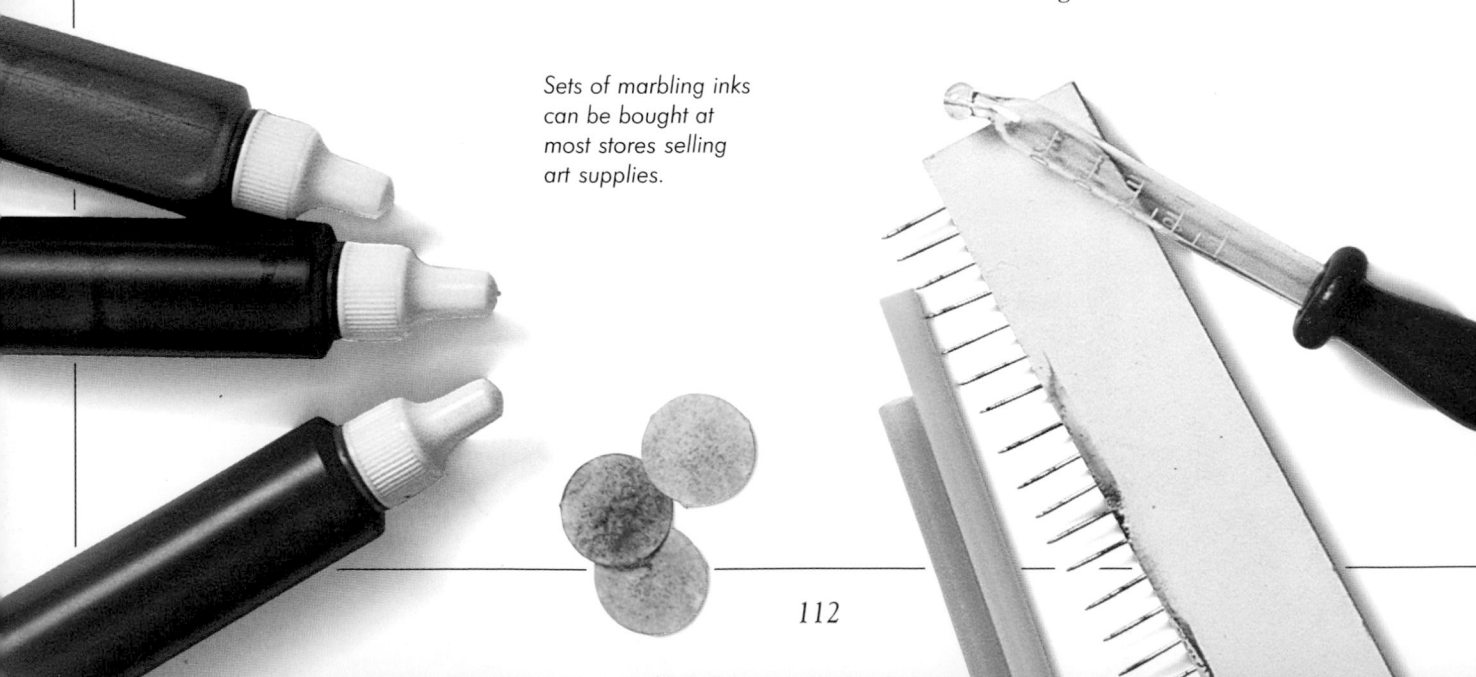

Sets of marbling inks can be bought at most stores selling art supplies.

1 ▲ *Fill a large tray two-thirds full with either water or size. Float marbling inks or fabric paints (according to the size) on the surface of the water, applying them with a brush or by using a drinking straw. Manipulate the floating colors with a skewer or a marbling comb.*

2 ▲ *Gently lay a piece of prepared white fabric, smaller than your tray, onto the inks. Make sure that no air bubbles become trapped beneath. Lift the fabric back in a rolling motion and lay it on newspaper to dry. Skim a strip of newspaper across the tray to remove any traces of color before repeating the process.*

Fragments of silk, marbled with paint and coarse salt, can be used to make cards and jewelry.

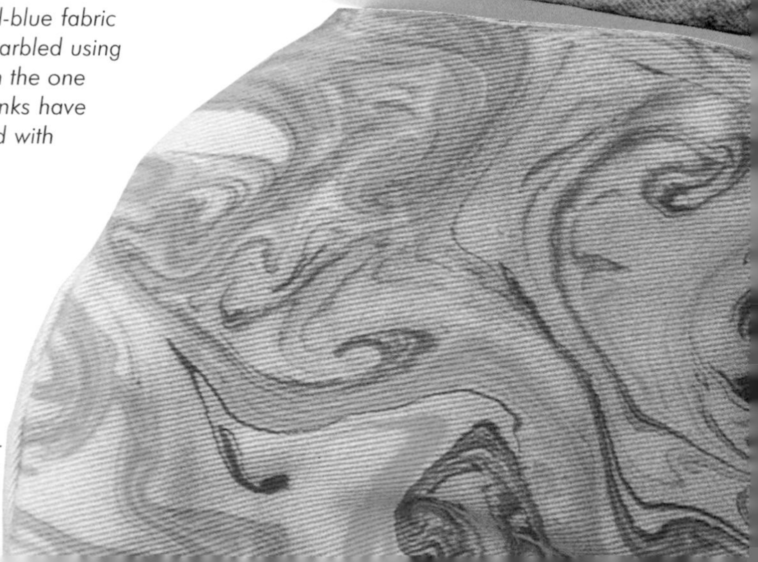

The red-and-blue fabric has been marbled using a comb. On the one below, the inks have been swirled with a skewer.

PROJECT 37

Salt Scarf

YOU WILL NEED
- silk
- silk paints
- coarse sea salt
- a needle & thread
- scissors
- paint brushes
- a frame
- an iron

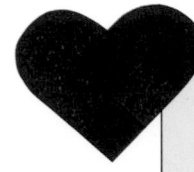

A sprinkling of coarse salt on wet silk paint produces a lovely mottled effect. The scarf can be made to any size you choose.

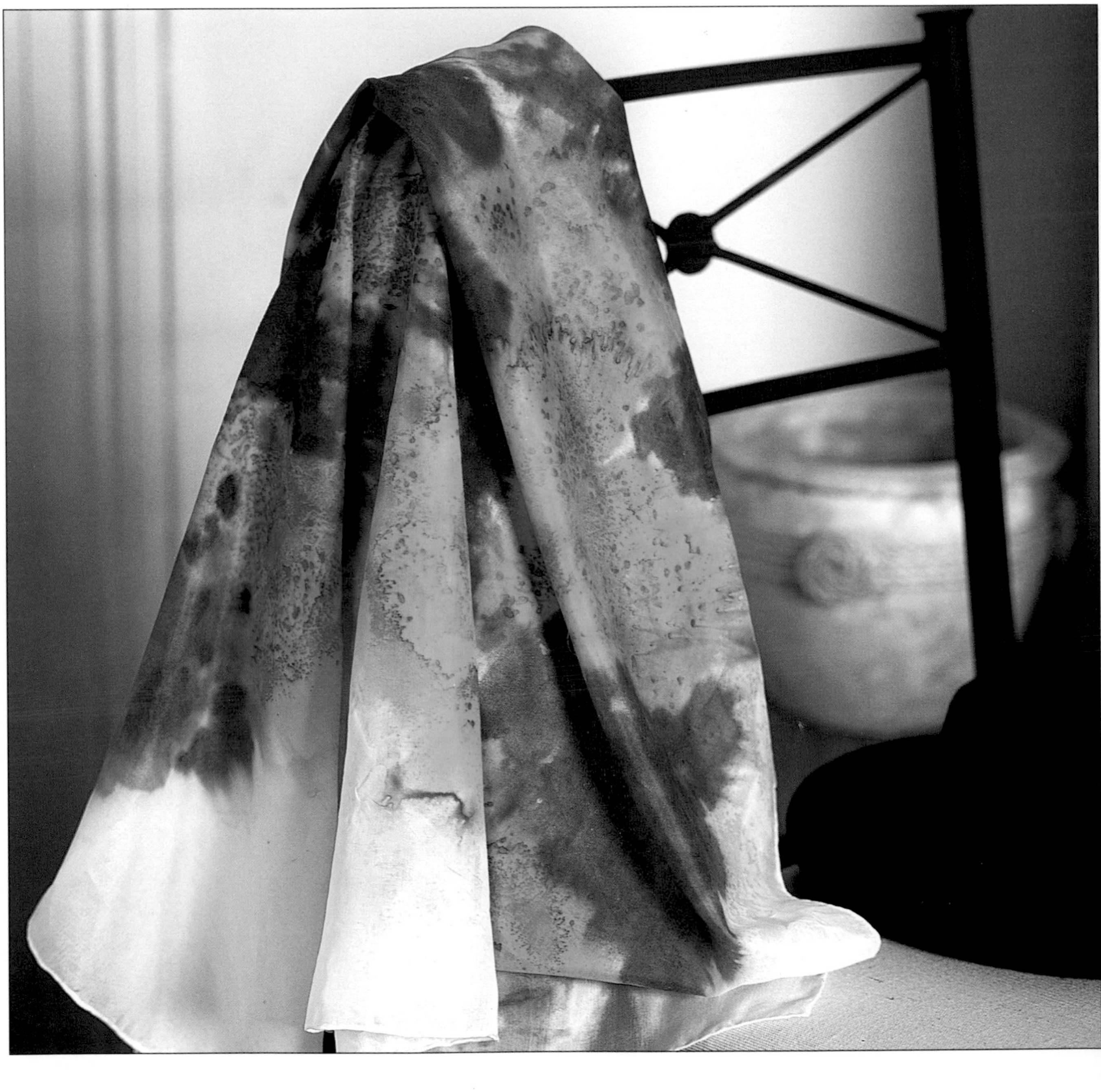

1 ▶ Handwash a square of silk to remove any sizing. Dry and press it carefully. With dampened fingers, roll the edge of the fabric and secure it with a series of tiny stitches to form a rolled hem. Hem all four edges.

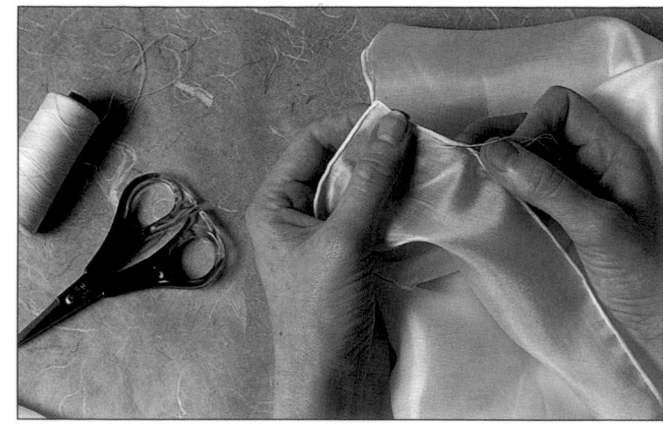

2 ◀ Stretch the silk onto a frame. Pin it onto a large rectangular frame or fix it in an embroidery or quilting frame. The silk should be held taut. If the frame is not large enough o hold the full scarf, complete the marbling section by section, allowing the paint to dry each time.

3 ▶ Test the silk paints on a scrap of silk; add a little water to make the colors less intense. If the paint does not spread well, brush some water onto the silk before applying paint. Apply paints to the fabric with different brushes, dabbing the paint in several places.

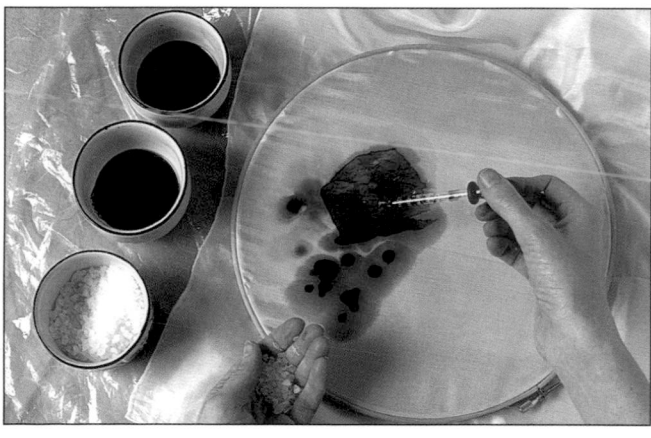

4 ▶ While the paint is still wet, sprinkle coarse salt onto the painted area. When the silk paint is quite dry, brush off the salt and fix the paint according to the manufacturer's instructions.

PROJECT 38

Marbles Bag

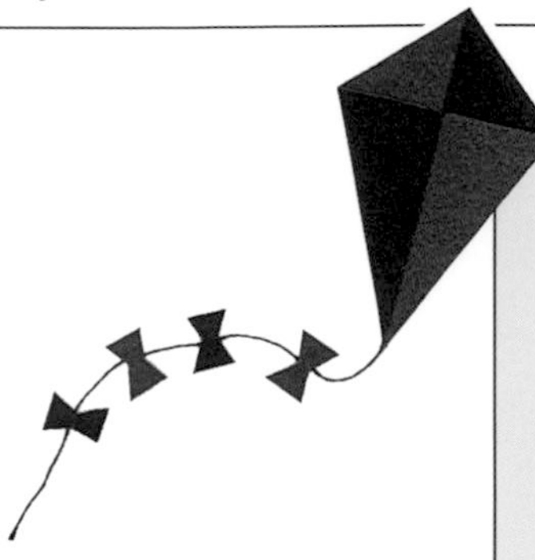

A really good collection of marbles deserves a good bag, and what better way to decorate it than with a swirl of marbling?

YOU WILL NEED
white fabric
lining fabric
marbling inks
a tray
a straw or brush
a skewer
decorative cord
sewing equipment
a sewing machine

1 ◀ Fill a large tray two-thirds full with water. Float marbling inks, either by gently touching the surface of the water with a brush or by using a drinking straw to drop ink. If the ink sinks, push a scrap of paper under the water. When the paper rises, drop ink onto it. Swirl the floating ink gently with a skewer or blow on it.

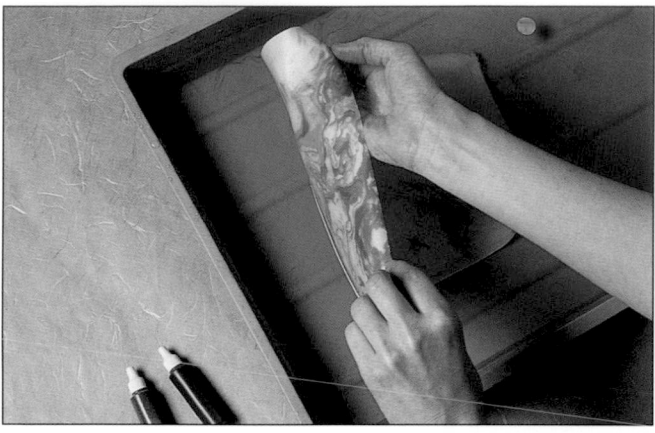

2 ◀ Gently lay a piece of white fabric, smaller than your tray, onto the inks. Make sure that no air bubbles become trapped beneath. Lift the fabric back in a rolling motion and lay it on newspaper to dry. Repeat with at least two more pieces of fabric.

3 ▶ Cut a marbled circle with a diameter of 5 " and two marbled 8 " squares. Lay the squares together, right sides facing, and sew a 1/2 " seam along one edge, stopping 21/2 " short of the end. Join the circle to the long edge of the squares and sew the other side seam, again stopping short at the top.

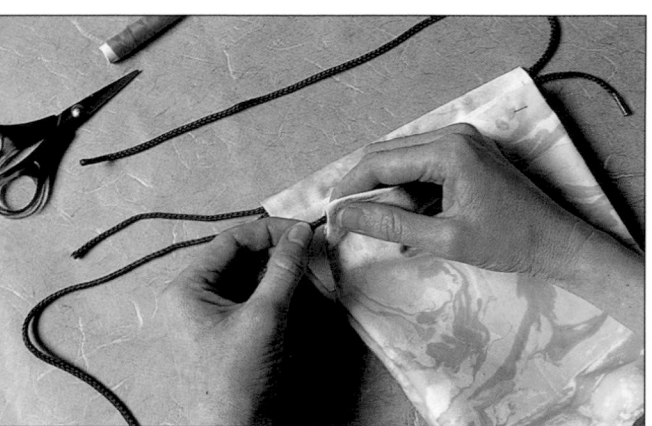

4 ◀ Cut lining pieces and sew a matching bag. Place this in the marbled bag, wrong sides facing. Turn and sew a 1/2 " hem along the top of the marbled bag. Trim the top of the lining slightly lower than the marbled bag. Turn the latter over by 3/4 ", covering the lining edge, and sew along the top and bottom of the casing, turning in the ends neatly. Cut two 24 " lengths of cord and thread them through the casings in opposite directions, so that the two sets of ends lie at opposite sides. Knot each pair of ends.

PROJECT 39

Lampshade

As this project won't need to be washed, you can decorate it with simple oil-on-water marbling. The single color lends the shade an air of elegance.

YOU WILL NEED
muslin
oil paint
a large tray
a straw or a brush
turpentine
thin cardboard
a lampshade frame
bias binding
scissors
glue

1 Cut pieces of muslin slightly smaller than your tray. Fill the tray with water. Thin some black oil paint with a little turpentine. Use a drinking straw or a brush to release droplets of paint onto the water's surface and then swirl the paint gently. Lay a piece of muslin on the water and roll it off again. Leave fabric to dry.

2 Lay the lampshade frame on a sheet of thin cardboard. Slowly roll the frame and mark the lines of both edges to map out the lampshade shape. Allow a 1" overlap at one end. Cut out this shape and a matching piece in marbled fabric, sewing two pieces together if necessary.

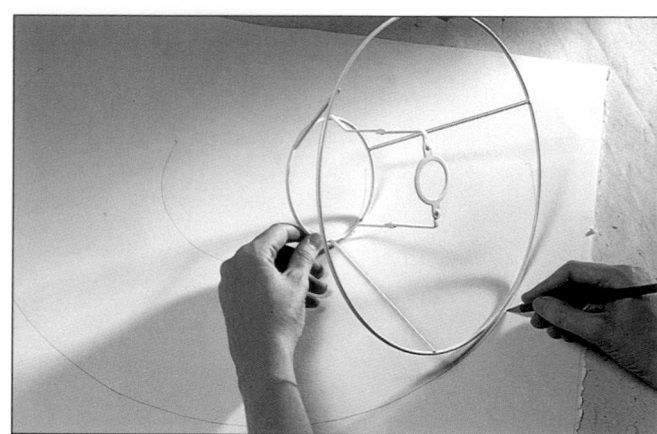

3 Fit the cardboard section onto the frame and glue the overlapping ends. Spray the back of the marbled section with adhesive and fix it onto the card, glueing down the overlap.

4 Cut black bias binding to fit around the top and base. Fold it over the wire frame and glue it onto both the shade and the frame. To improve the appearance, you may wish to glue another length around the inside top of the shade.

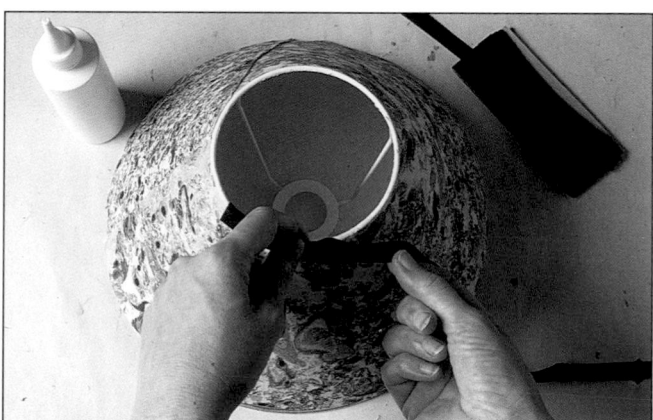

Printing

For some people, the thought of painting a design freehand is a little daunting. A good solution to this lack of confidence is to print or stencil a design. This allows you to plan the design before the paint bottle is even opened. These methods also allow you to paint that design repeatedly, with some success assured each time and with a minimum of effort.

Before you proceed, it is worthwhile reading the notes in the chapter on painting, as the same basic information applies to any of the paint techniques.

Printing is the use of an object, known as a "block", to transfer paint onto a surface. The block can be any number of things—leaves, half an orange, a clothes peg—as long as it has a surface which will hold paint. Prints from these simple blocks can be arranged in a pattern on the fabric. More complex designs, however, can be achieved if the block is shaped in a design. A potato, cut in half, can be cut to make a motif. Felt shapes can be mounted on a piece of stiff cardboard. Impressions can be carved in cork, linoleum and erasers, leaving raised sections which receive the paint or ink and so print when pressed on the fabric. Craft linoleum can be bought in small sheets from most stores which sell art supplies, along with sets of cutting tools.

When designing a relief print, remember that the print will be a mirror image of the design on the block. This is important if you plan to include writing in your design. A repeat design for a border will need to match at both ends, as in the pattern in Project 42.

Test the print on scrap fabric before working on your project, as you may need to adjust the consistency of the paint. Don't be too concerned about getting the print perfect: an interesting effect is achieved when the prints are slightly erratic. Different results can be achieved by dipping the block in the paint or by brushing paint onto the block. The block should be pressed firmly onto the fabric; a roller may help to apply an even pressure.

Rollers, lino-cutters and special paints for printing on fabric are all available for enthusiasts.

Printing blocks
Almost anything which has
a flat surface can be used as
a printing block. Examples
shown here include a carved
eraser, pieces of foam rubber,
a felt shape, ivy leaves and
a bought rubber stamp.

PROJECT 40

Peg Bag

Almost any object with a flat surface can be used as a printing block. Here, the humble clothes peg proves its worth.

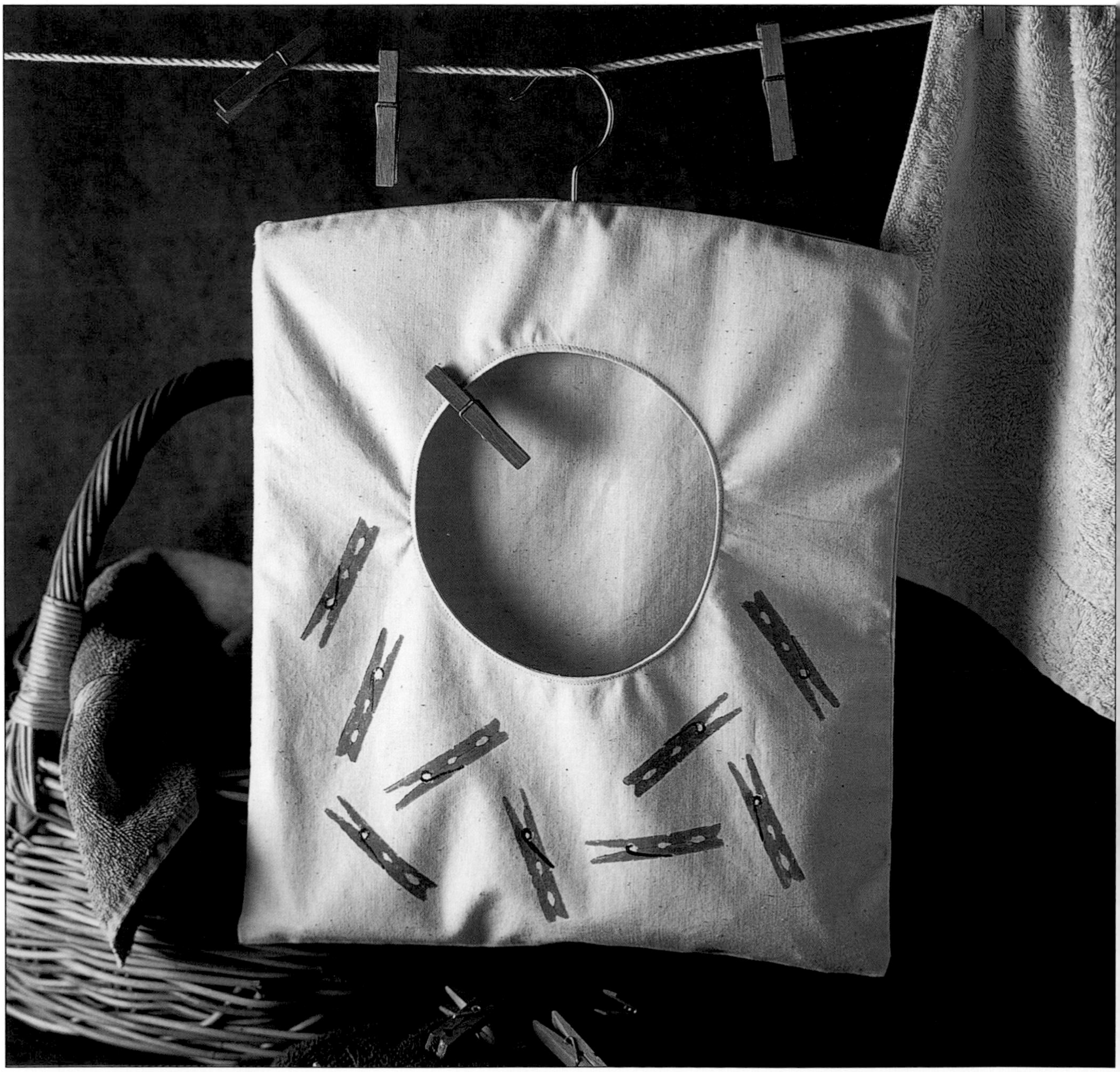

1 ▶ Cut a piece of fabric 2 " wider than the clothes hanger and twice the required length. Cut another piece the same width but half the length. Use a small saucer to mark a circle on this piece, towards the top. Lay the two pieces together and pin around the circle, then flip back the top layer for printing the design.

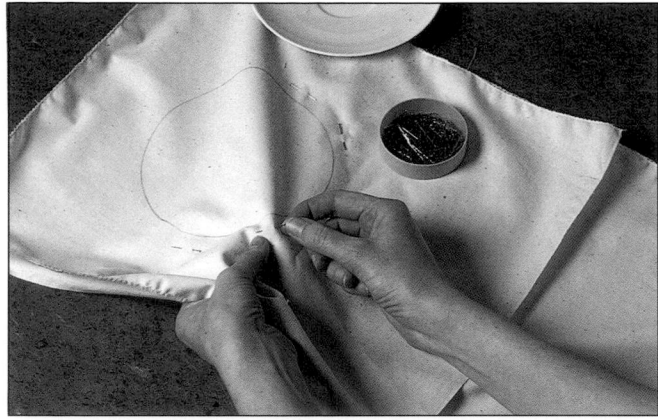

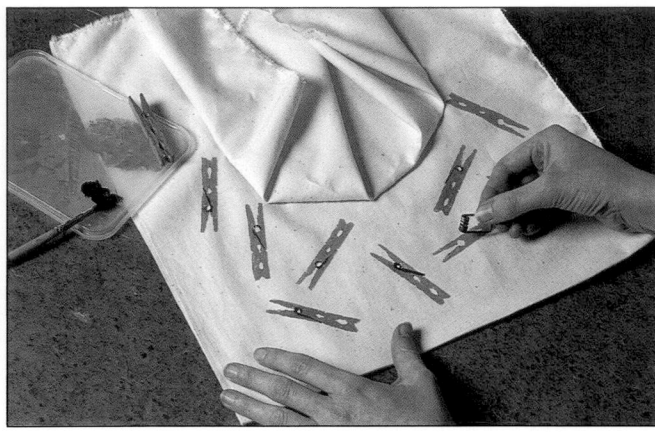

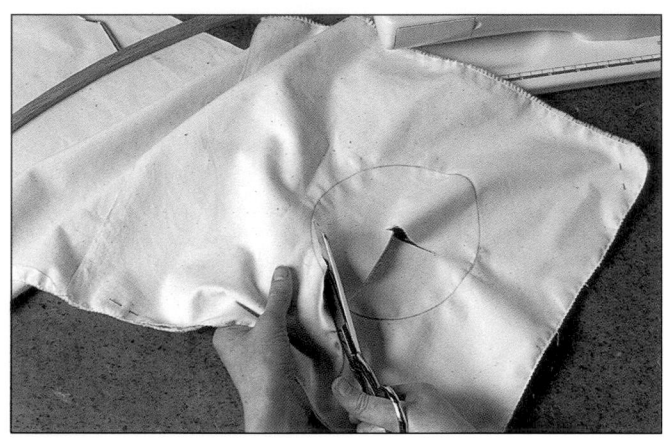

2 ▲ Remove the metal spring from a wooden clothes peg. Glue the halves together, making sure that the side surface is quite flat. Coat this with paint and press it onto the bottom layer of fabric, below the pinned circle. Make multiple prints, recoating the peg each time. When the paint is dry, apply black paint with the spring.

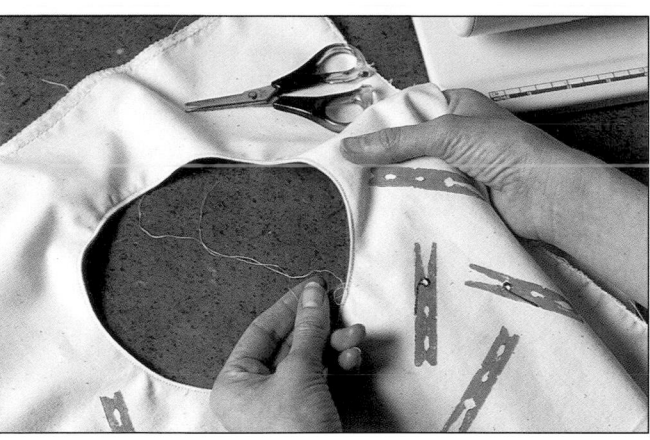

3 ▲ Flip the front section down and machine sew around the circle, securing the two layers of fabric together. Cut through both layers and trim within the circle, $1/4$ " from the stitching.

4 ◀ Turn the front section through the hole and press the seam flat. Machine a row of stitches $1/8$ " out from the edge of the hole, preventing the concealed raw edges from fraying. Sew the base of the short section to the middle of the long section.

5 ▶ Lay the clothes hanger along the top with the printed face lying down and mark the shape of the arms. Fold the fabric at the center, right sides facing, and sew a $1/2$ " seam along the edges and along the marked top, leaving a gap for the hook. Turn the bag and insert the clothes hanger through the hole.

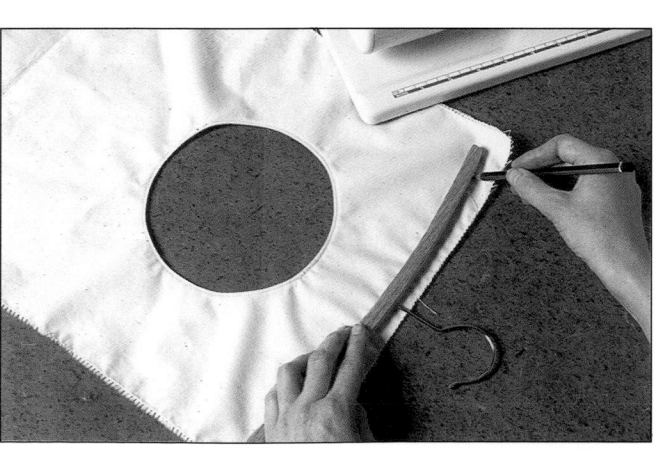

PROJECT 41

Blocks

YOU WILL NEED
thick foam sponge
a serrated knife
a ruler
a felt pen
non-toxic fabric paints
cotton fabric
sewing equipment

Soft blocks are great fun for toddlers. Make sure you use non-toxic fabric paints, as they will probably be taste-tested more than once.

1 ◄ Mark and cut 3" square cubes from a thick sheet of foam sponge, using a felt pen and a serrated knife. Select offcuts of sponge which have one smooth surface and draw simple motifs on them. Cut these out, either with scissors or the serrated knife.

2 ◄ Wash and iron pieces of cotton fabric in several different colors. Cut 4" squares; you will need six squares for each block. Dip the smooth face of a sponge motif into non-toxic fabric paint and press it onto scrap fabric to test. If necessary, adjust the amount of paint loaded on the motif and press it evenly onto a fabric square.

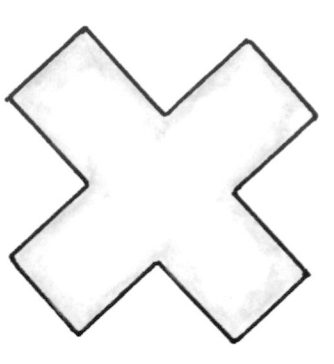

3 ► Print on all the fabric squares, allow the paint to dry and then fix it according to the manufacturer's instructions. Staystitch around all the squares. Lay two squares together, right sides facing, and sew a ½" seam along one edge. Open the double section and lay two more squares on top, face down, then sew a seam at each end to form a chain of four squares. Lay this face up and lay another square face down at one end.

4 ► Continue sewing seams that join the edges of the squares, creating a box shape, until all but three seams remain unsewn. Snip a small triangle off each corner so that the seams will not be too bulky. Turn the box inside out and insert the foam block. Pin the "lid" of the box down and handsew the remaining three seams.

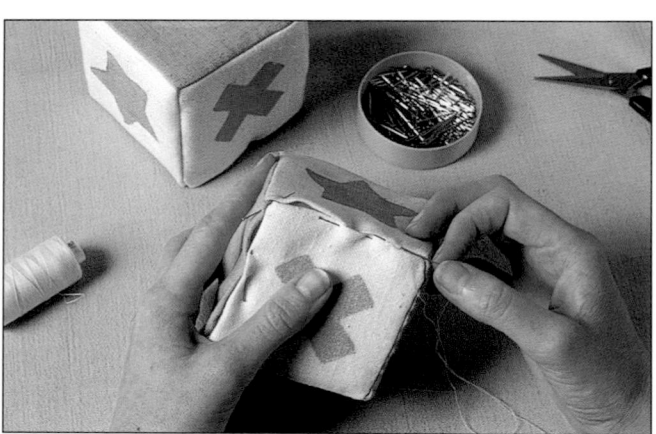

PROJECT 42

Roman Wrap

YOU WILL NEED
pale fabric
linoleum
lino cutters
tracing paper
a pencil
fabric paint

Linoleum is a wonderful material to work with and enables you to print quite detailed designs. This key pattern is used to good effect on a classic shawl.

1 Lay tracing paper on the pattern and trace over the lines with a soft pencil. Turn the tracing over and lay it on a strip of linoleum. Run a blunt tool or the end of the pencil over the lines, transferring the design onto the linoleum.

2 Mark the uncolored areas of the design with pencil and use a U-gouge or a scalpel to cut away the material from these areas. Cut carefully, so that the lines of the pattern are sharp and the curves are smooth.

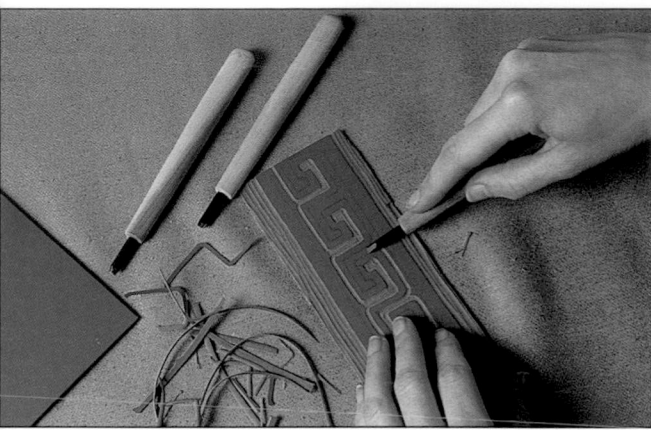

3 Prewash and dry a square of fabric. Apply fabric paint to the linoleum block with a roller or a brush, or simply by laying the block face down in a shallow pool of paint: each method gives a different result. Press the block onto scrap fabric and adjust the amount of paint if the print lacks clarity. Lay the block on the fabric and press the back with your palms.

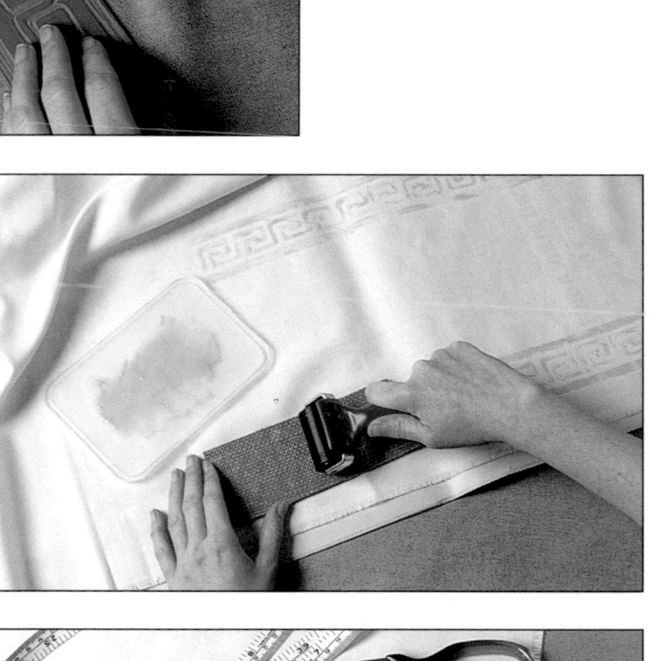

4 Make a series of prints around the fabric square, carefully aligning each before you press the block down. Print another series in the center. Fix the paint as per the manufacturer's instructions. Make a fringe by teasing out threads from each edge of the square.

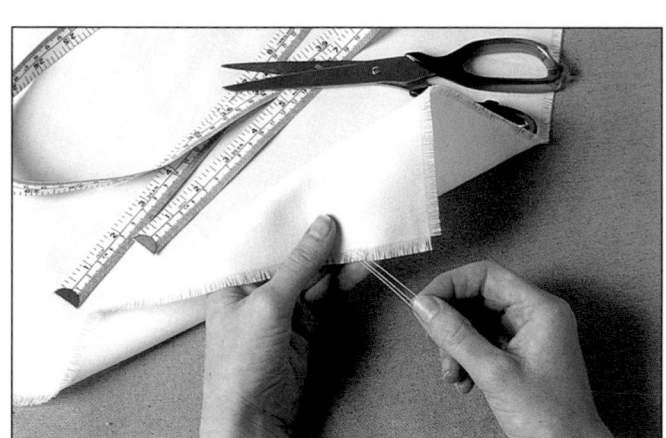

Stenciling

There are several easy methods of making a repeat pattern on fabric: printing is one, stenciling is another. A stencil is a design, cut in cardboard or acetate, which is held against the fabric while paint is applied. You can buy ready-cut stencils, but it is very easy to cut your own.

A stencil design must have "bridges" built into it to hold the stencil together: some images will need to be simplified or stylized to suit this painting technique. Stencils can be cut from clear acetate, which allows you to see the pattern below when cutting and is easy to position on the fabric for painting. Acetate can be difficult to cut without slipping so you may prefer to use waxed cardboard, available from some craft stores, or plain thin cardboard. If you use the latter, apply a coat of varnish after cutting the stencil as this will extend its life.

A stencil brush has short, stiff bristles of an even length. Alternatively, you could use a sponge to apply the paint to large areas, giving a mottled effect.

It is important that both the fabric and the stencil on it lie perfectly flat. Masking tape can be useful to hold the stencil in place.

Keep the paint reasonably thick; if it becomes too thin, it will seep under the edges of the stencil and blur the design. The paint need not be applied evenly and an interesting texture can be achieved by letting the brush run out of paint as you work.

If you wish to paint a design in two or more colors, you can choose to use the one stencil or you can cut a stencil for each color and apply them in stages. If you use this second method, make sure you position each stencil carefully or the colors will be out of alignment.

Use stencils to apply repeat border designs or to decorate sets of things, such as table linen or nursery furnishings. File old stencils in batches of designs for children, for Christmas and so on, so that they can be easily found and used again.

Oil-based stencil crayons can be used on fabric projects which will not require washing.

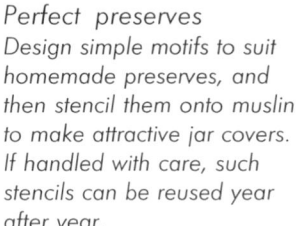

Perfect preserves
Design simple motifs to suit homemade preserves, and then stencil them onto muslin to make attractive jar covers. If handled with care, such stencils can be reused year after year.

◄ To cut a stencil, lay a piece of acetate over your design. Cut the design with a sharp knife, taking care not to slip and make unwanted cuts. Hold the blade upright and cut into the waste area.

Stencils can be used in combination with other fabric painting techniques to produce a range of unusual effects.

◄ Position the stencil on the fabric and tape it in place. Load the brush with fabric paint and dab any excess on scrap material. Dab the brush down onto the stencil, working inwards from the edges of the design. Remove the stencil and wipe it clean for reuse.

PROJECT 43

Mug Mats

These mats bear a traditional American schoolhouse design. Spices, added to the wadding, will produce a pleasant scent when hot mugs are placed on the mats.

YOU WILL NEED
top fabric
backing fabric
wadding
tracing paper
acetate
a knife, mat & ruler
tape
fabric paint
a stencil brush
sewing equipment

1 For each mug mat, cut a 6 " square of top fabric and a matching square of backing fabric. Trace the pattern onto paper, lay it on a cutting mat and tape a piece of acetate over it. Use a ruler and a sharp knife to cut out the colored areas of the design.

2 Tape the acetate stencil over a top square. Dip the stencil brush in a small amount of fabric paint and dab it onto the fabric square, taking care not to let paint seep under the stencil. Apply paint in each section of the stencil. Remove the stencil and allow the paint to dry. Fix the paint according to the manufacturer's instructions.

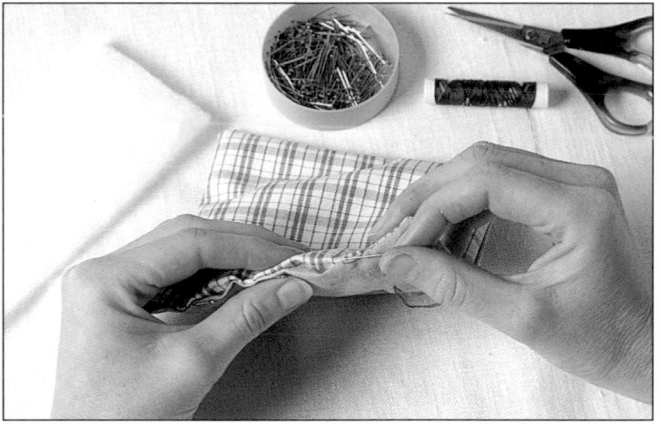

3 Lay a stenciled square and a backing square together, right sides facing, and sew a ½ " seam around three edges. Turn the mat right side out. Cut a square of wadding to fit, insert it in the square, and slipstitch the fourth side closed.

4 Handsew large tacking stitches in embroidery thread, running around the square ½ " in from the edge. This will secure the wadding in place and add a finishing touch.

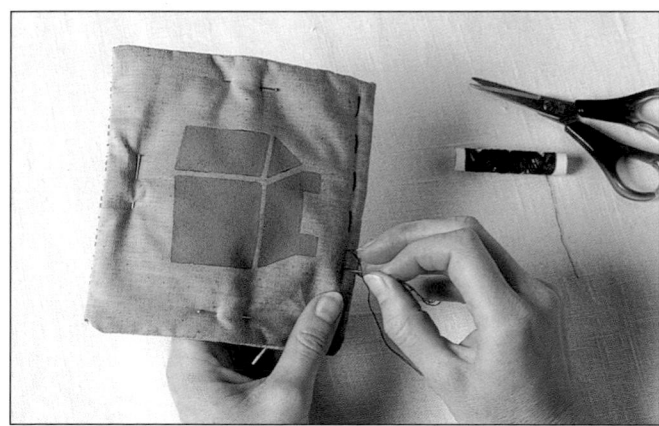

PROJECT 44

Card Cloth

For the card sharks amongst your friends, here is a stunning cloth to cover the card table and set the mood.

YOU WILL NEED
pale fabric
tracing paper
acetate
a knife, mat & ruler
tape
fabric paints
a stencil brush
sewing equipment
a sewing machine

1 Wash the fabric thoroughly to remove any size, then hang it to dry and iron it well. Cut a square of fabric to suit your card table: this cloth is 30 " square. Staystitch the edges and press a ¼ " fold, then press a ½ " hem and machine sew around all four edges.

2 Trace the shapes onto paper in a diamond arrangement. Lay the tracing on a cutting mat and tape a piece of acetate over it. Use a ruler and a sharp knife to cut out the colored areas of the design. Cut a series of ½ " boxes on a separate piece of acetate.

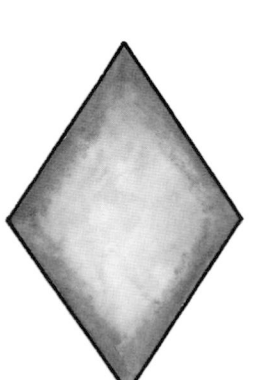

3 Position the stencil over a corner of the cloth and tape it in place. Dip the stencil brush in a small amount of red fabric paint and dab it onto the appropriate section of the stencil, taking care not to let paint seep under the stencil. When the red paint is dry, apply black paint to the other sections of the design.

Remove the stencil and allow the paint to dry. Fix the paint according to the manufacturer's instructions.

PROJECT 45

Number Chart

Stenciling is an ideal way to paint multiples of a design.
If you're feeling ambitious, you could extend this
number chart to the count of ten!

YOU WILL NEED

muslin
colored fabric
tracing paper
acetate
a knife, mat & ruler
tape
fabric paints
a stencil brush
buttons
sewing equipment

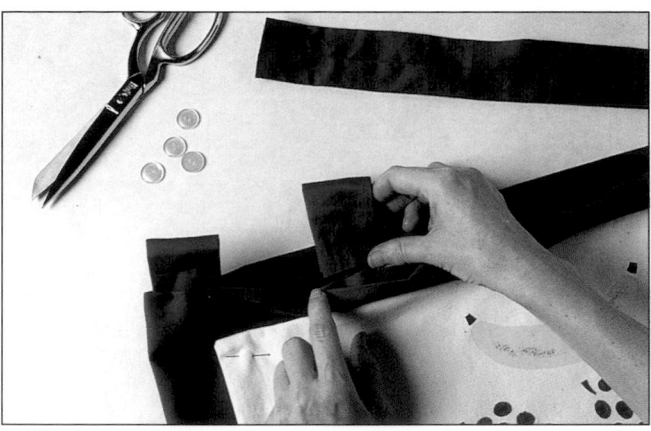

1 Prewash the muslin, then let it dry and iron it well. Cut two 16½ " squares of muslin. Trace the numbers on page 159 onto paper, lay this on a cutting mat and tape a piece of acetate over it. Use a ruler and a sharp knife to cut out the numbers. On another piece of acetate, cut out the shapes below. Mark guidelines on the muslin with tailor's chalk. Tape the numbers stencil onto the muslin and stencil them in one colour of fabric paint, moving the stencil as required. Stencil the fruit shapes in various colors, taking care not to touch any area that is still wet. Start in the middle of each row and work outwards.

2 Lay the muslin squares together, right sides facing, and sew a ½ " seam, leaving a gap for turning. Trim corners, turn and slipstitch the gap closed. Cut two 20 " squares of colored fabric and repeat the above procedure, leaving the fourth edge unsewn. Cut a 5 x 24 " strip of colored fabric. Fold it lengthwise and sew a ½ " seam to form a long tube. Turn the tube right side out with the handle of a wooden spoon and press. Cut this into five equal sections and fold each one to form a loop. Position the loops in the opening of the colored bag and sew it closed. Position the stenciled muslin bag on the colored bag and secure in place with buttons at each corner.

135

Embroidery

It did not take very long, in the development of civilization, before the stitching once used to join pieces of fabric was given a decorative purpose. Greek fabrics dating back to the 4th century BC have been found embellished with satin and chain stitches. The Romans referred to the art as "painting with a needle" which reveals how highly they valued it.

In the centuries since, an enjoyment of embroidery has ben shared by the rich upper classes and the poorest peasants. The fabrics on which they stitched differed, the one working on satins and silks, the other on coarsely woven cloths. Those who had leisure stitched on all sorts of furnishings and clothing, while those with less time and fewer materials embroidered specifically for a wedding trousseau or other special festivity. Regional differences also arose, such as the use of small mirror pieces in Indian needlework, but foreign trading brought many local techniques to different countries.

As a result, the present-day embroiderer has an immense range of stitches and styles from which to choose. The main choice is between counted embroidery—using specific stitches such as cross stitch on an evenly woven fabric—and free embroidery, in which there is no restriction on the stitches and fabrics used. In the former, a charted pattern is transferred onto the fabric by counting. In free embroidery, a complex design can be marked on the fabric and used as a guide.

Choose a needle and thread to suit the ground fabric. Crewel needles, which have a long oval eye and a sharp point, are suitable for free embroidery; cross stitch should be worked with a rounded needle which does not split the threads of the fabric. A frame can be useful to keep the fabric taut.

Fabrics with an even weave are necessary for counted embroidery stitches such as cross stitch.

STITCHES

Satin stitch
Work a row of parallel stitches very close to each other, keeping an even tension.

Stem stitch
Work from left to right. Keep the thread to the left of the needle and make small even stitches; increase the angle of the needle for a wider effect.

Bullion stitch
Pick up fabric the size of the required stitch but do not pull the needle through. Twist the thread around the needle. Hold the twists and pull the needle through, then insert it back at the starting point.

Backstitch
Working from right to left, make a short stitch to the right and bring the needle out to the left, the same distance from the starting point.

Cross stitch
Make a series of diagonal stitches and then return along the row, making a second series of diagonal stitches to form crosses.

The letters on this scissors case are worked in counted cross stitch.

Here, a felt mouse, a baby's vest and even a pair of gardening gloves are decorated with bullion stitches.

PROJECT 46

Napkins

YOU WILL NEED
linen
embroidery thread
tracing paper
a pencil
sewing equipment
a sewing machine

*A personal initial on a napkin turns a useful item into
a charming gift. These monograms are embroidered in
a combination of satin stitch and stem stitch.*

1 Cut 16 " squares of linen in a color to suit your tableware. Staystitch around the edges of each piece. Turn over ¼ " at each edge and iron the fold. Trim the corners at an angle. Turn over another ¼ " and machine sew the hem, giving special attention to the corners.

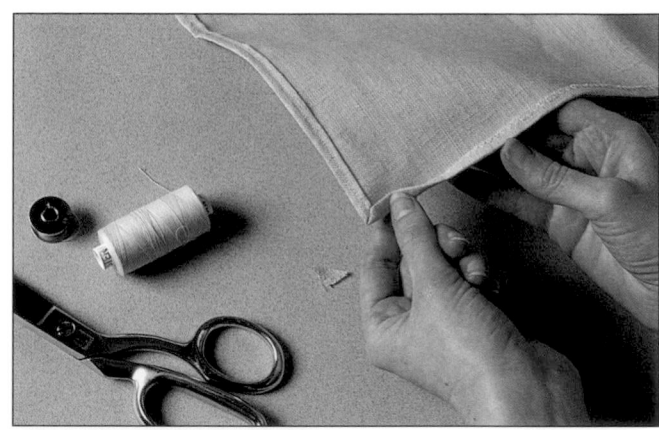

2 Lay a piece of tracing paper over the pattern on pages 156-7 and draw the appropriate letter. Trace the letter outline neatly with pencil or tailor's chalk onto the right side of a napkin corner as shown. If necessary, tape the tracing to a window and place the hemmed napkin over it to trace.

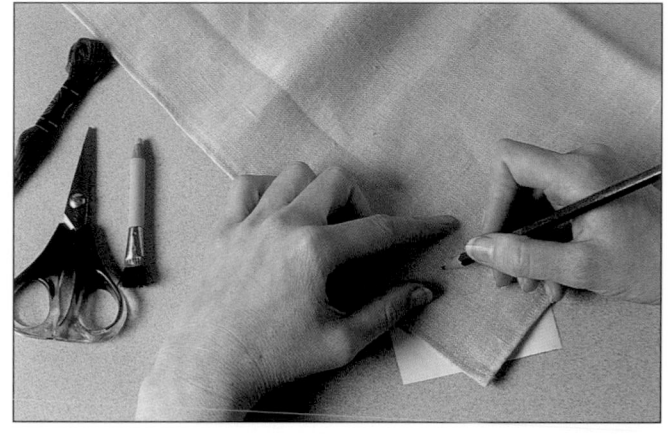

3 Thread a sharp needle with embroidery thread and, holding the napkin right side up, bring the needle through from the back at a suitable starting point. Secure the tail of the thread with the stitches that follow. Both satin stitch and stem stitch are explained on page 137.

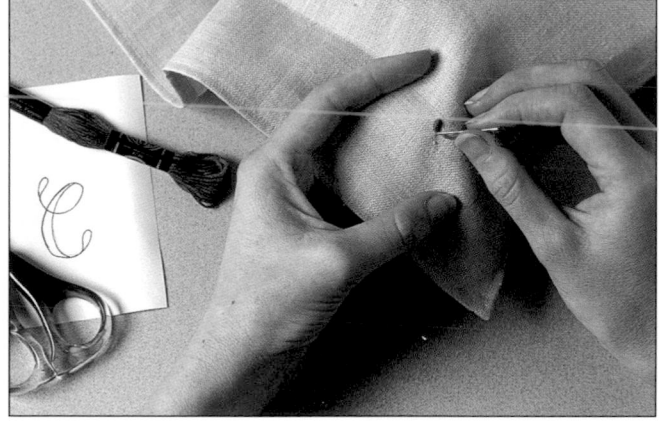

4 Work the traced design carefully, using stem stitch to form narrow lines and satin stitch to fill in areas. Stitch an appropriate mono-gram in the corner of each napkin.

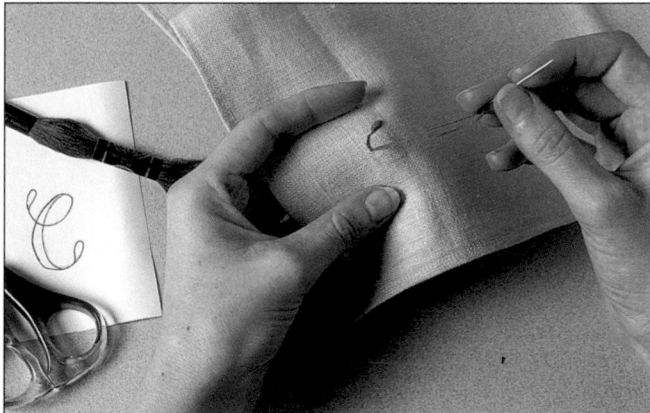

PROJECT 47

Shoe Shapers

YOU WILL NEED
heavy fabric
embroidery threads
lavender
fiber filler
fine needles
sewing equipment

Your best shoes deserve special attention: these pretty sachets will keep them in perfect shape and smelling sweet.

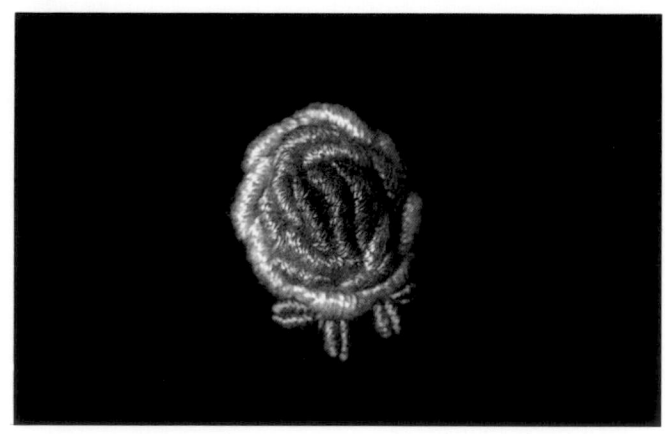

1 Using bullion stitch (see page 137), stitch a rose and leaves onto heavy fabric such as velvet. For the petals, use a No.5 needle with six strands of thread and make eleven twists per stitch. For the leaves, use a No.8 needle with three strands and make six twists per stitch.

DMC 3731
deep pink

DMC 3733
mid pink

DMC 3713
pale pink

DMC 3052
green

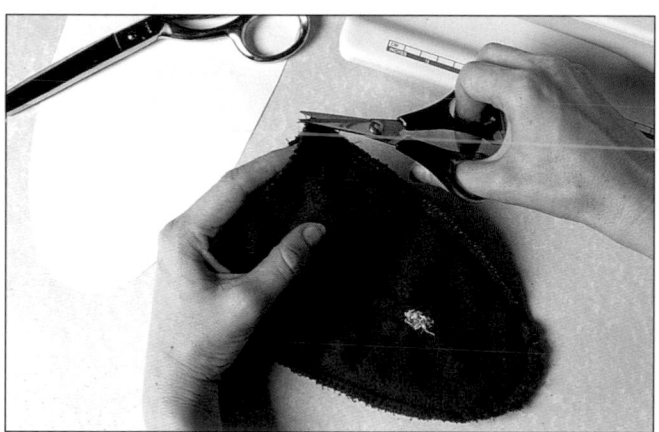

2 Trace the pattern on page 159 and cut a paper template. Cut two fabric pieces for each shaper, one with a rose in the center. Staystitch all edges. Lay an embroidered piece on a backing piece, right sides facing, and sew a ½ " seam around the curved edge. Turn the shaper right side out.

3 Push some fiber filler into the toe of each shaper, then add a heaped spoonful of dried lavender and cover it with more fiber filler. Fold the top edge in by 1½ " and tie two narrow ribbons tightly around the neck.

PROJECT 48

Finger Puppets

YOU WILL NEED
14-count Aida fabric
backing fabric
embroidery threads
a blunt needle
sewing equipment

These farmyard characters are simple to cross stitch and will have great child-appeal. The stand is made by pushing dowel into a drilled wooden base.

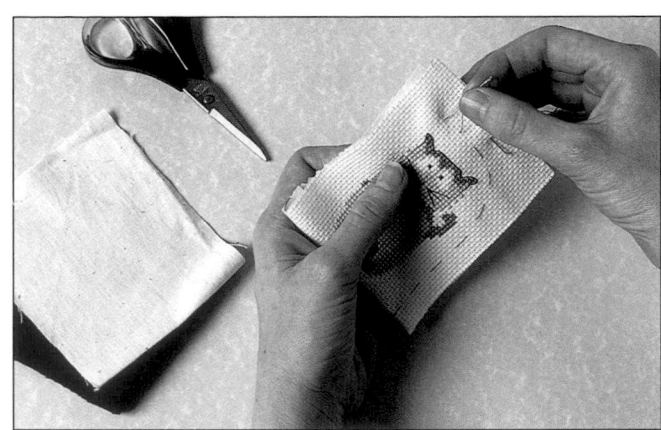

1 Cut 6 x 4 " of 14-count Aida for each puppet. Using two strands of thread, stitch crosses (see page 137), calculating the position on the fabric from the chart. Work the whole pattern, referring to the key and counting stitches on the chart. Add backstitching in a single strand of black.

2 Cut a colored backing piece and two lining pieces. Lay the embroidery face down on a lining and sew along the base, ¼ " below the bottom row of cross stitches. Do likewise with the backing and other lining. Turn the sections so the seams are concealed. Tack around the design and trim, then stay-stitch the raw edges.

3 Place the two sections together with the bases aligned and the cross stitching and colored fabric facing each other. Sew the layers together, using the tacked outline as a guide. Turn the puppet right side out.

KEY	Symbol	DMC No.	Symbol	DMC No.
	■	310	U	444
	Z	352	▲	606
	O	353	−	741
	*	414	+	922
	X	415	•	white

Beadwork

In earlier times, when all beads were shaped by hand, a garment or furnishing decorated with beads was a sign of wealth and power. From the Americas to the Far East, people adorned their clothes with beads of wood, bone, shell and glass.

Today, beads are readily available in most places where you can buy fabrics. In many cities, there are also specialist bead stores which boast an amazing array of beads. Beads are also sold by mail order in most countries.

Beads come in all shapes and sizes, giving you almost unlimited opportunities for decoration. Most beads are drilled through the center, but drop beads are often drilled through the top and serve as a good end bead in a fringe. Glass and plastic beads can be washed with a garment, but avoid using natural stones. When planning a beaded project, keep in mind the weight of the beads, and the number you will require to finish it.

Sketch your rough design onto scrap paper or graph paper before transferring it onto fabric. If the design is too complex to be marked on fabric with tailor's chalk, copy it onto thin tracing paper and stitch this onto the fabric, tearing it away once the design is marked with tacking lines or the beads are sewn in place.

Complex beading should be worked on fabric before it is made up. If the fabric is thin, line it with a heavier material and secure the beads to both layers. Use a strong thread or double thread, matching the fabric or the beads as closely as possible. You will need a thin needle with a tiny eye to fit through the bead holes, so a needle threader may also come in handy! Always secure the beading thread with two small stitches on the reverse of the fabric. The method you then use depends on whether the beads are to be spaced apart or set in a continuous line. Instructions are given on the next page.

Beading can add a sparkle to plain fabrics, or be used to embellish or highlight a printed design. A border decoration of beads gives a finished appearance to an item. Beads can be sewn on randomly or in an established design; you could use tiny beads to work someone's initials. A beaded fringe adds an air of elegance to scarves, wraps and even lampshades.

Keep your collection of beads in some sort of order using an empty egg carton, some film cannisters, or a purpose-bought bead box.

◀ Single beads, or those spaced widely apart, can be stitched on fabric with a backstitch. Secure the thread and bring the needle up. Thread a bead onto the needle and then make a bead-sized stitch back from right to left. Bring up the needle in front of the next bead's position.

Bead shapes
Above, from left to right: glass rocailles, discs, long bugles, drop beads, glass pebble beads.

▶ To couch beads, secure a double thread on the reverse of the fabric. Thread on a number of beads and position the string as desired. Secure another needle and thread near the start. Make a small stitch over the first thread, between the first and second bead. Repeat, working along the beads.

Beading can be as simple as a ring of round beads on a delicate lavender bag, or as complex as this heavily beaded purse.

PROJECT 49

Decorations

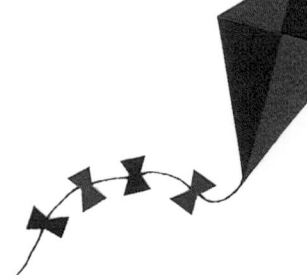

YOU WILL NEED
*colored fabrics
fiber filler
ribbons
small glass beads
a marker
sewing equipment*

*A few well-placed "rocailles" or seed beads add
a sparkle to these decorations, ideal for hanging
on a tree or from a mantelpiece.*

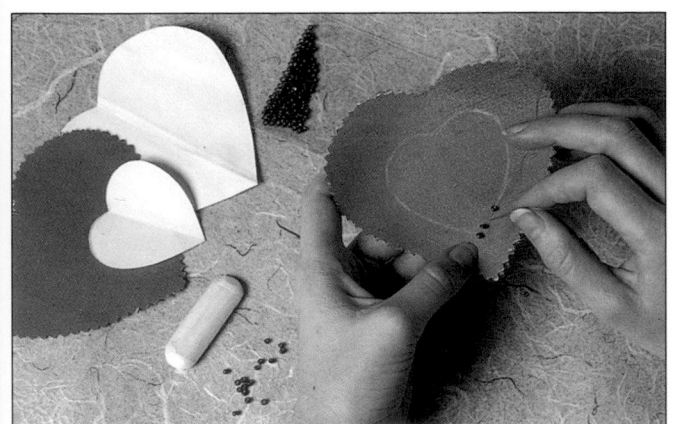

1 Enlarge the patterns by 200% and transfer onto colored fabrics. Cut two pieces (with an extra seam allowance) for each decoration. Secure thread of a matching color at the reverse of a fabric piece. Bring the needle up, pick up a bead and make a small backstitch. Bring up the needle a short distance in front of the previous stitch, pick up another bead, and so on.

2 Lay the two beaded sections together, right sides facing, and sandwich a loop of ribbon between them so that the ends of the ribbon are aligned with the top edges of the fabric shapes. Sew a ½" seam, leaving a small gap for turning. Snip darts at the sharp corners and turn the decorations right side out.

3 Fill the decorations with polyester fiber so they are plump but not overfilled. Slipstitch the gap closed with small, neat stitches.

Beaded Cover

YOU WILL NEED
fine fabric
small round beads
larger drop beads
a saucer
sewing equipment

Beaded jug and food covers are both practical and decorative. Remember that the larger the cover, the more beads you will need!

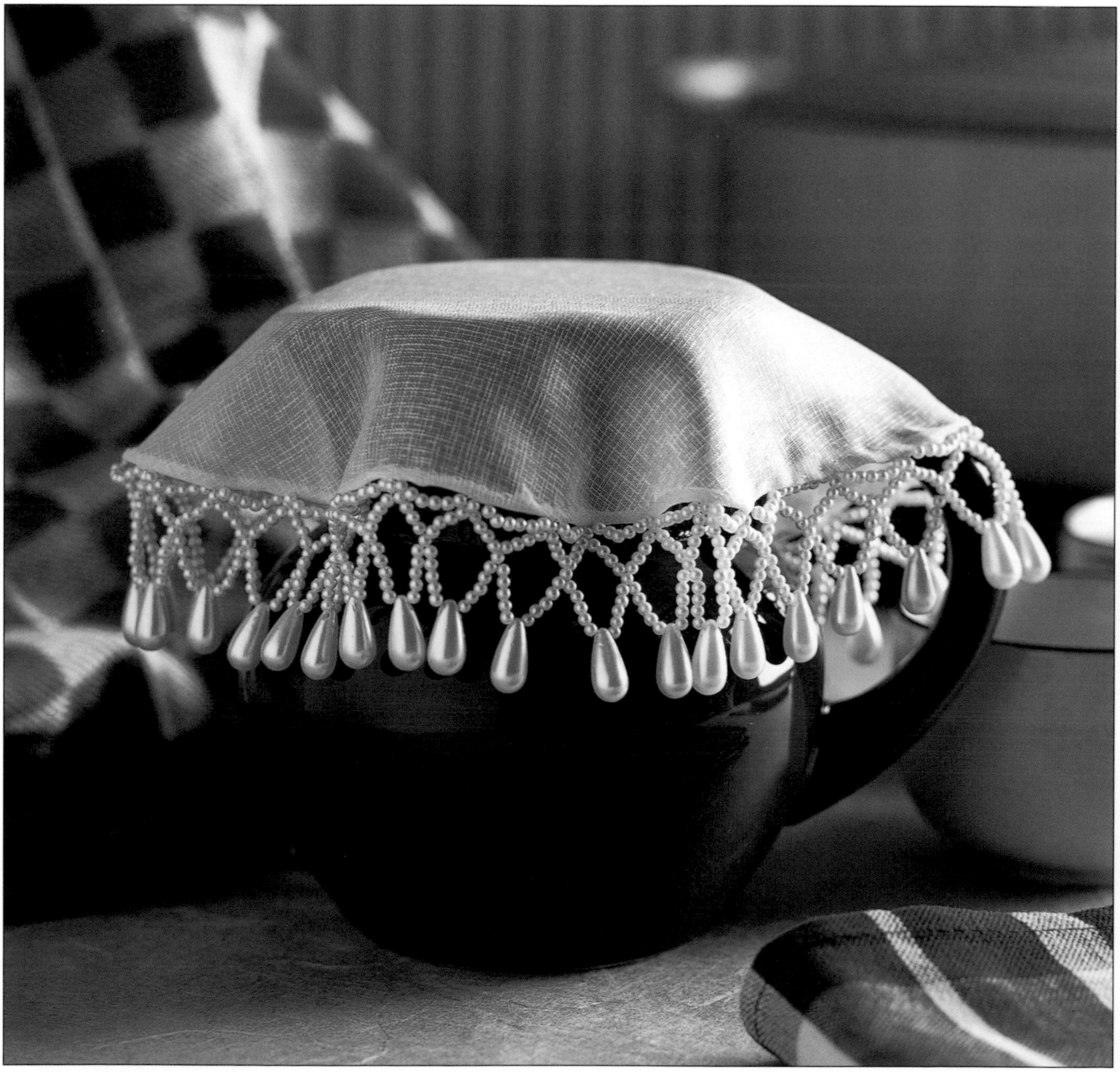

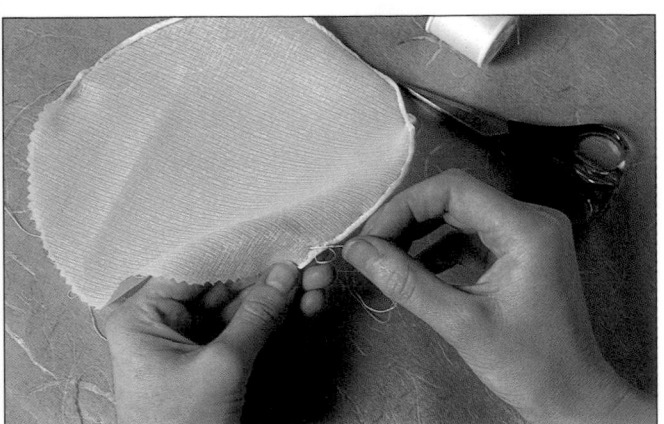

1 Choose a fabric which is lightweight and attractive. Mark and cut a circle with a 7 " diameter, or to suit your own needs. Carefully roll the edge of the circle and secure it with a series of stitches to form a rolled hem. When the hem is complete, secure a fresh thread at any point on the hem.

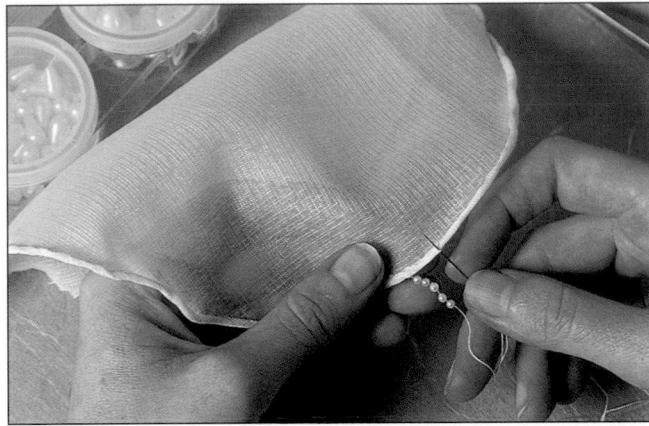

2 Thread six small beads onto the needle. Make a stitch further along the hem so that the beads hang loosely along the edge of the fabric.

3 Take up eleven small beads, followed by a drop bead (here, a teardrop shape) and then take up eleven more small beads. Thread the needle through the first bead in this step and make a stitch into the hem, to form a bead loop with the drop bead at the bottom.

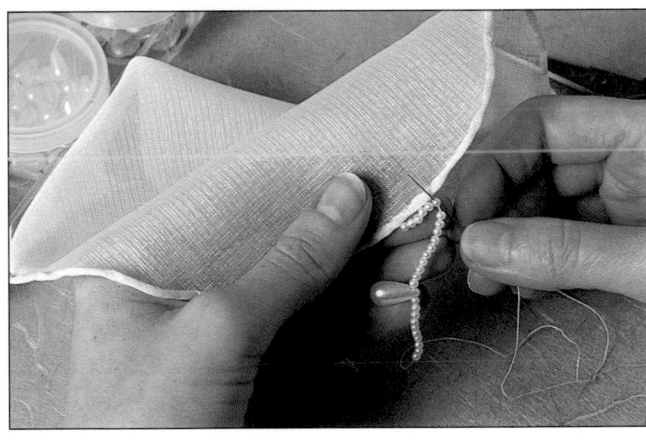

4 Repeat step 2, then take up five small beads and catch the sixth on the previous loop. Take up another five small beads, then a feature bead, and continue as above in step 3. Repeat this pattern right around the hemmed circle.

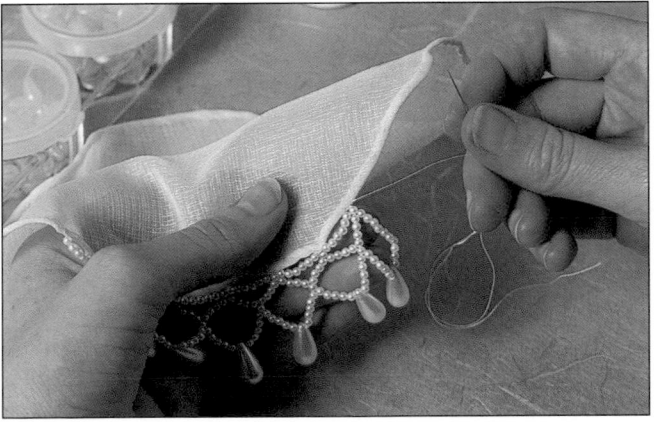

PROJECT 51

Evening Bag

*Gold on black is a striking combination and this little bag
will be sure to catch the eye. The elaborate beading is
easier to work than it may appear.*

YOU WILL NEED
black velvet
black lining fabric
wadding
round gold beads
long gold beads
tracing paper
a pencil
sewing equipment
a sewing machine

1 Cut a 14 x 10 " piece of velvet. Trace the beading pattern on page 159 onto thin tracing paper. Pin the tracing onto the velvet so that the center of the design is 3½ " from one short edge. Tack with a white thread along the lines of the design. Tear away the tracing, leaving the tacking lines in place.

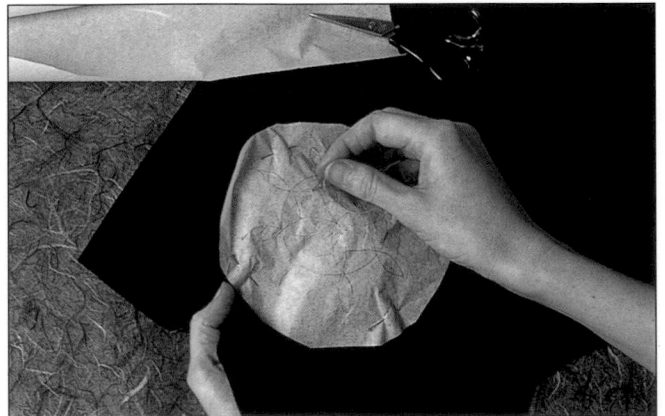

2 Work the spiral design with long beads, securing them in place with a gold or black couching thread (see page 145). The bicone beads used here are ¼ " long and fit the design well. Backstitch the round beads in place around the spiral and in the center. When the beading is complete, remove the tacking threads.

3 Cut an 8 x 10 " piece of velvet and lay this on the unbeaded end of the large piece. Curve the corners, as shown on page 159. Cut a 2 x 21 " side band and stay-stitch all pieces. Pin the band along the curved edge of the smaller section, right sides facing, and sew. Align the unbeaded end of the large section and attach to the band likewise.

4 Cut lining and make up a matching bag. Insert this in the velvet bag, wrong sides facing, with wadding in between. Turn the edges of both bags in and slipstitch the lining in place, leaving a gap at both sides. Cut 48 " of cord, loop the ends and insert them in the sides. Sew them in place and then slipstitch the gaps closed.

Gift Giving

A handmade gift is always warmly received and often sincerely treasured. The simple act of making something with a particular person in mind makes it instantly special.

This book is filled with projects which make wonderful gifts and which can be adapted slightly and made into unique presents. Think about friends' preferred colors or a child's favorite animal motif and make your choice of fabric or design accordingly. Make gifts that will fit into people's homes: if they like the country style, use a checked fabric in strong colors; if their decorating scheme is more formal, choose a fabric in a pastel shade.

Several fabrics are traditional gifts for specific wedding anniversaries: cotton is appropriate for the second year, silk or linen for the twelfth year, and lace for the thirteenth. If you're not a stickler for tradition, however, a gift of fabric is fine at any time!

Fabric makes a wonderful (and entirely recyclable) packaging material. If you use a scarf or a fabric bag, the wrapping can even become a part of the gift. A few ideas for presenting gifts are featured on these pages.

Use a silk scarf to wrap a piece of jewelry or a small token.

A potpourri of pine sprigs, cloves and cinnamon in a festive fabric sack makes a fragrant gift.

Black organza and
a gold ribbon make
a striking wrapping
for sweets.

Dress up a bottle
in a muslin bag
painted with vine
leaves.

Home made
preserves look
even better with
a fabric covering.

Making Tags & Cards

When we think of greeting cards, we tend to think of paper rather than fabric. Many of the techniques in this book, however, can be used to make wonderful cards and tags.

A simple piece of embroidery makes a thoughtful handmade card for a special occasion. Methods such as printing and stenciling are suitable for making multiple cards for such festivities as Christmas. Cards can even be decorated with small beads—just make sure they will fit in an envelope!

To frame a piece of fabric in a card, use a three-panel mount such as the two shown on the far right of page 155. Blank mounts can be bought in craft stores or you can make

your own by folding a piece of cardboard into three panels, cutting a window in the center panel, and securing the fabric behind it.

To make cards speedily, decorated fabric can simply be glued on the front of a two-panel card. Cut motifs from patterned fabrics, or use pinking shears to trim edges quickly. Scraps of marbled or painted silk can become miniature works of art when fringed and presented on a card.

Gift tags can be adorned with felt motifs, scraps of lace, small ribbon bows, or whatever you choose. Tags can simply be cut from fabric, as they tend to have a shorter lifespan than cards. Choose a plain fabric and write on it with pen or fabric paint.

Clockwise:
A folded gift tag framing a
scrap of painted silk; a tulip
motif embroidered in satin
stitch; a three-panel mount
framing a patterned fabric;
a card made of woven ribbons;
felt on a label-shaped tag;
flower designs cut from fabric
and glued onto card.

Letter patterns for Project 46

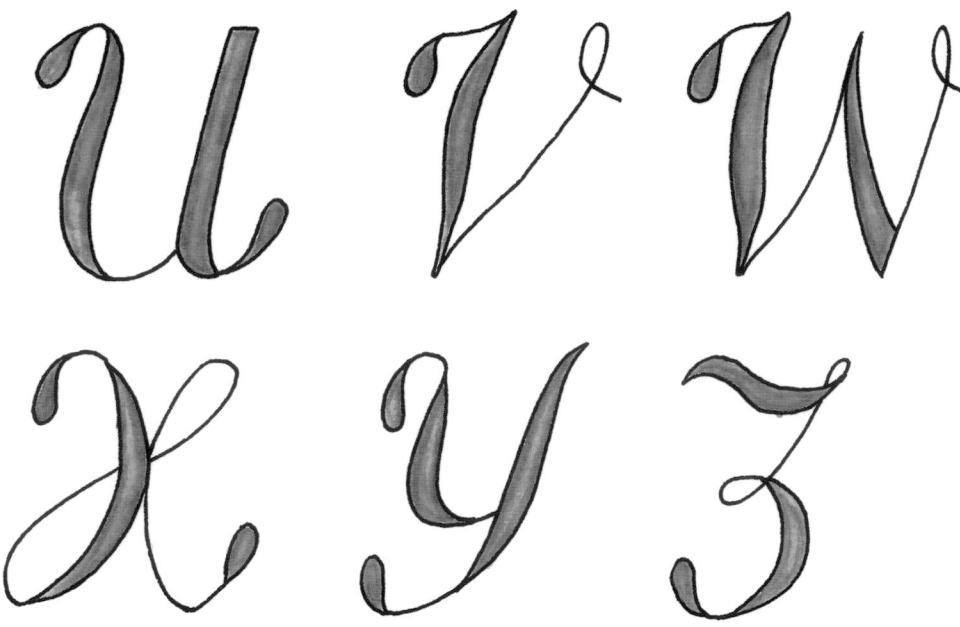

Numbers pattern for Project 45

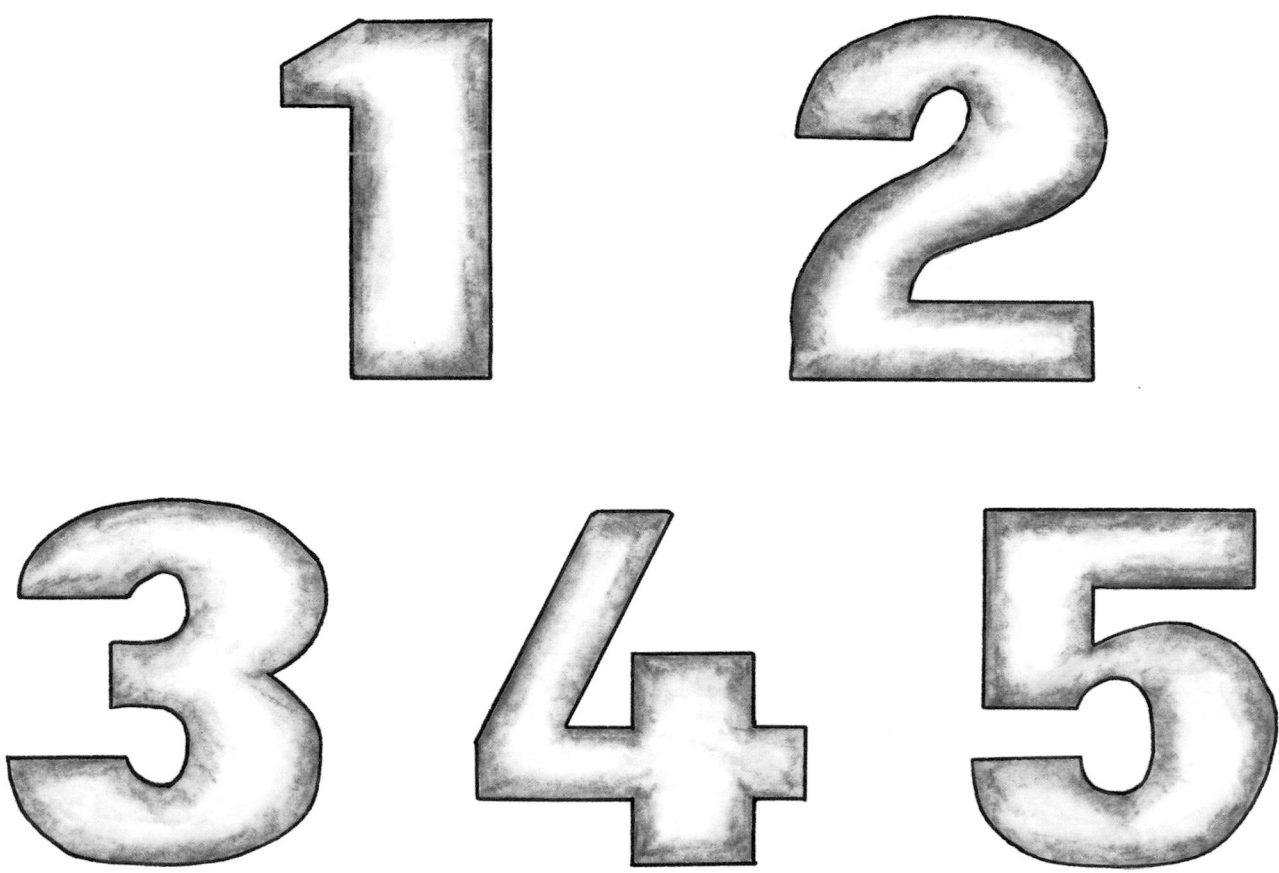

Doll & dress patterns for Project 9

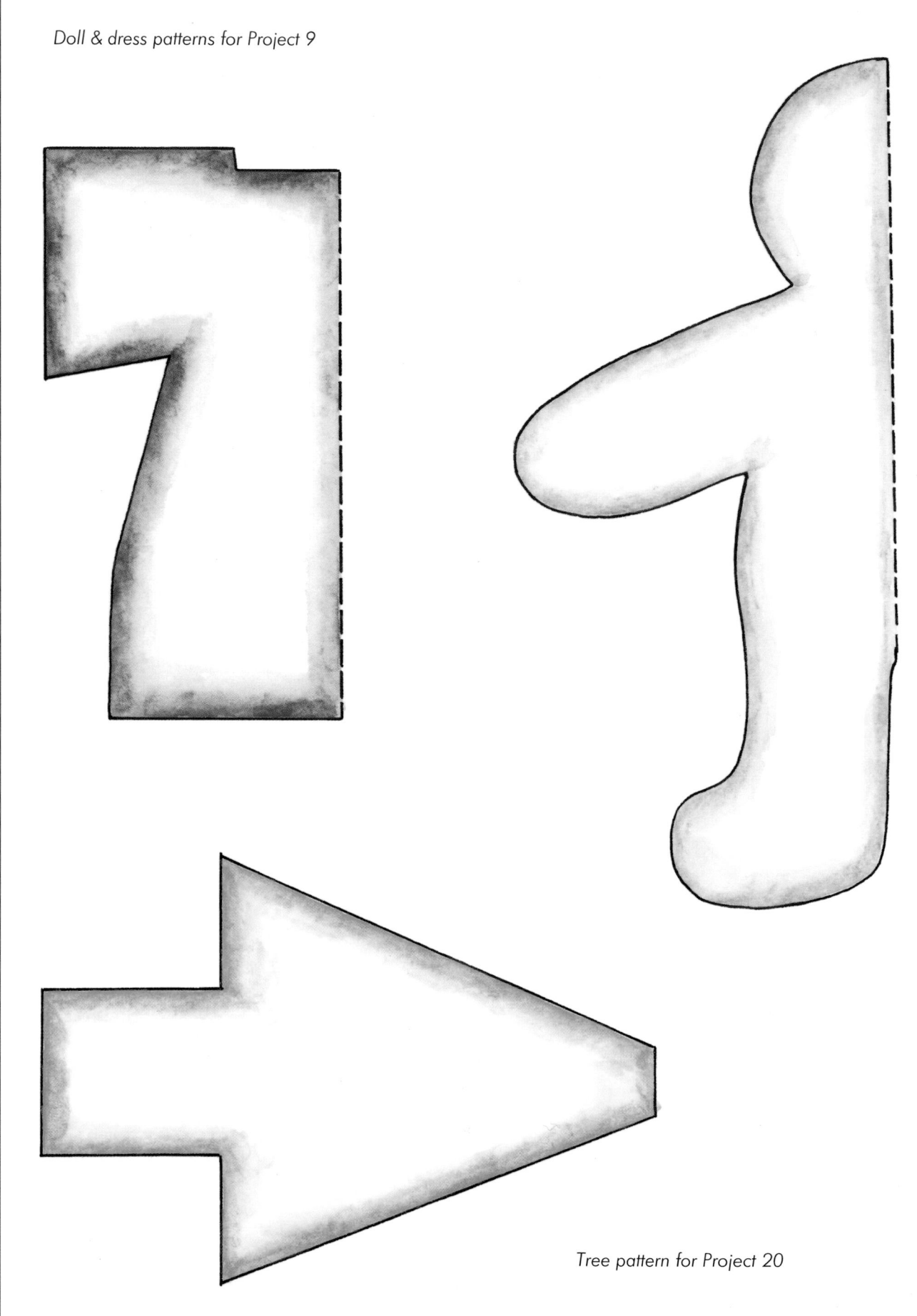

Tree pattern for Project 20

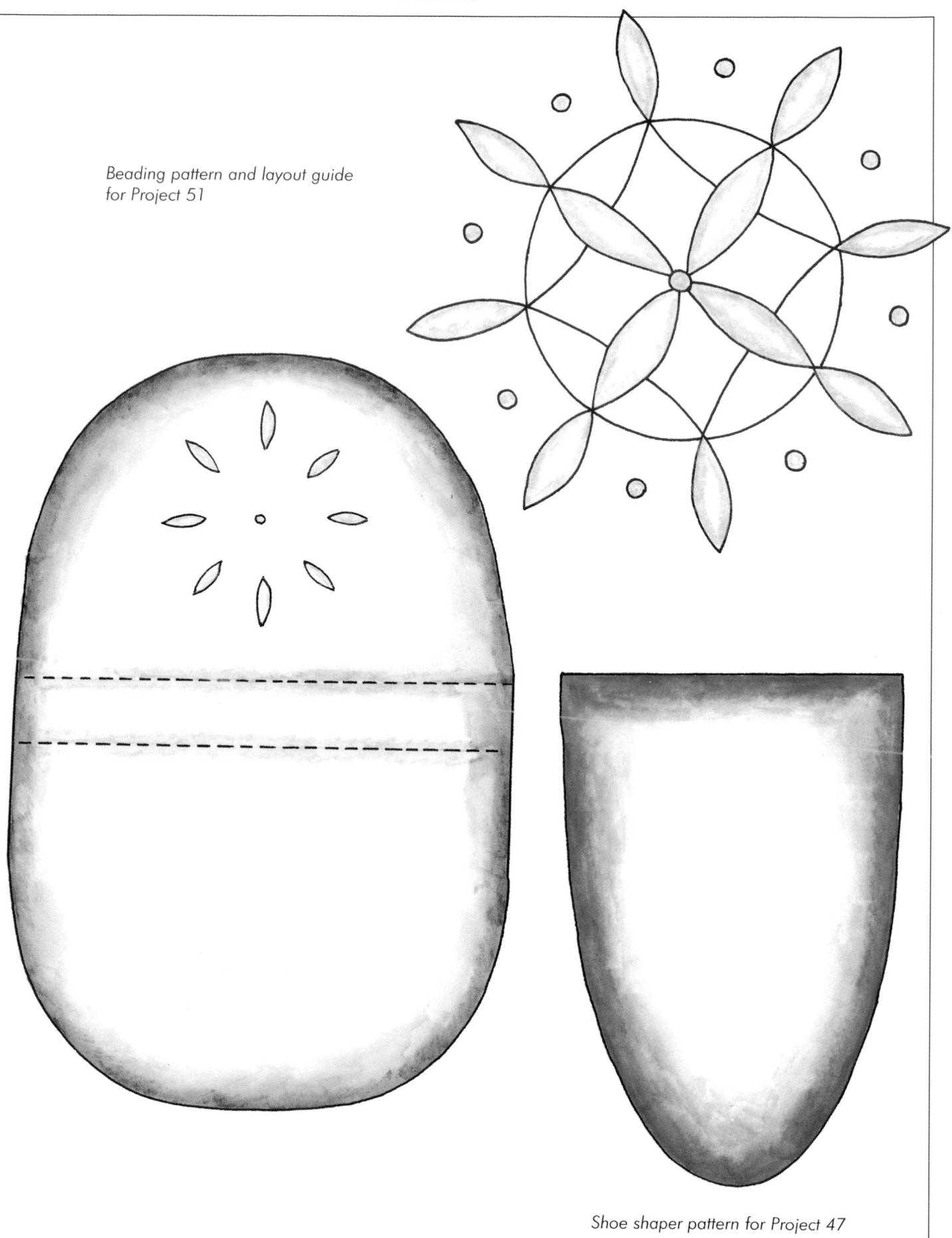

Beading pattern and layout guide for Project 51

Shoe shaper pattern for Project 47

Index

accessories
    evening bag 150-1
    hat 30-1
    scarf 114-5
    tie 108-9
    vest 36-7
    wrap 126-7
advent tree 68-9
appliqué 24, 32, 64-71, 72-3, 88
bargello 46-7
batik 105, 110-1
beads 36-7, 88, 97, 144-151
bookmark 20-1
boxes, covering 88, 94-5
bullion stitch 137, 140-1
bunting 106-7
canvaswork 40-7
card table cloth 132-3
cardboard loom 17
cards 65, 100-1, 154-5
cartonnage 88-95
chateleine 89
Christmas ideas 33, 68-9, 84-5,
 146-7
clothes hanger covers 50-1
cot cover 70-1
cot linen 54-5
cross stitch 136-7, 142-3
cushions 46-7, 74-5, 98-9
decorations 146-7
dyeing 104-111
embroidery 32, 88, 136-143
equipment 10-11
fabric
    grain 12
    paints 10, 96, 112
    preparation 13

    sculpture 80-7
    types 8-9
felt 9, 24-31, 64-5
felting 25, 31
Florentine stitch 41, 46-7
flowers, fabric 25, 49, 81
food cover 148-9
glasses case 42-3
greeting cards 65, 100-1, 154-5
hot water bottle cover 76-7
jewelry roll 78-9
lace 32, 36-7, 48-51, 54-5
lampshade 118-9
marbling 88, 112-9
needlepoint 40-7
notebook 90-1
ojos mobile 18-9
paint techniques
    marbling 88, 112-9
    printing 24, 120-7
    salt marbling 112-5
    silk painting 97, 100-1, 112-5
    spattering 98-9
    stenciling 128-135
patchwork 32, 56-63, 72, 88
patterns, transferring 14
peg bag 122-3
pen holder 86-7
pencil case 66-7
picture frame 92-3
pillows 74-5, 98-9
pin cushion 58-9
pot holder 110-1
potpourri sack 82-3
printing 24, 120-7
quilting 64, 71, 72-9
ribbons 15, 17, 32, 48-55

salt marbling 112-5
satin stitch 137, 138-9
Scottish stitch 42-3
sewing techniques 15
shoe shapers 140-1
silk painting 97, 100-1, 112-5
spectacles case 42-3
stenciling 128-135
stocking 84-5
tableware
    braided mat 34-5
    cutlery roll 26-7
    mug mats 130-1
    napkins 138-9
    tablemat 22-3
tassels 80, 85
tea cozy 62-3
tent stitch 41, 44-5
tie-dyeing 105, 108-9
tissue sachet 49
toys
    blocks 124-5
    clown soft toy 44-5
    cot string 28-9
    finger puppets 25, 142-3
    juggling toys 60-1
    marbles bag 116-7
    mobile 18-9
    number chart 134-5
    play mat 102-3
    play pillow 74-5
    rag dolls 38-9
    rosettes 52-3
    treasure chest 94-5
weaving 16-23
wrapping gifts 152-3
wreath 33

Acknowledgments & Sources

The publisher would like to thank the following for materials and items which appear in this book:
Dorothy Cleland - for Project 47, the gloves and mouse on page 137, and the towel on page 49.
Shirley Souter, Betty Marsh & Leonie Draper - for their help in making various projects in the book.

Craft With Class - for the vests on pages 65 and 137, and the handtowel on page 49. These and other items are available from the Rocks Market in Sydney.
Suzie Cheel - who made the tie on page 129.
Crafted Software - for the use of *Stitchcraft*, the program used to create charts on pages 45 and 143.